Manchester

A guide to recent architecture

...

David Hands and Sarah Parker
Photographs by Keith Collie

Manchester

A guide to recent architecture

• • • ellipsis

BRITISH LIBRARY CATALOGUING IN PUBLICATION
A CIP record for this book is available from the British Library

PUBLISHED BY ···ellipsis
2 Rufus Street London N1 6PE
E MAIL ...@ellipsis.co.uk
WWW http://www.ellipsis.com
SERIES EDITOR Tom Neville
SERIES DESIGN Jonathan Moberly

COPYRIGHT © 2000 Ellipsis London Limited

ISBN 1 899858 77 6

PRINTING AND BINDING Hong Kong

···ellipsis is a trademark of Ellipsis
London Limited

For a copy of the Ellipsis catalogue or
information on special quantity orders
of Ellipsis books please contact
Faye Chang
020 7739 3157 or faye@ellipsis.co.uk

Manchester: a guide to recent architecture

Sarah Parker and David Hands 2000

Contents

Introduction

This guide describes nearly 70 examples of the architecture that has shaped Manchester's social, cultural and economic identity over the last ten years. It has been written from two perspectives: one author was born and raised in Manchester; the other is an outsider looking in.

The city's identity has been significantly shaped by its strong Victorian infrastructure, largely connected to the new wealth brought by the industrial revolution. Then labelled 'Cottonopolis', Manchester's power and prosperity were generated by the flourishing cotton and textile industries which left a fine legacy of Victorian buildings, resulting in a city with a tremendous amount of civic pride. This heritage has lead to a vibrant and diverse city, the foremost financial, commercial and cultural capital of Britain's largest region outside London.

Manchester City Council's Urban Policy has encouraged quality, both in the conservation of historic buildings and in the design of new ones. Most projects promote sustainability and mixed-use, important elements of the policy. This is reflected in housing, offices, retail, education, and the arts, with each building narrating its new use, while renewing and enhancing the urban fabric. Many of the projects featured in this guide were designed by local architects and designers; it is also refreshing to witness the impact that 'outsiders' have had on the built environment.

Funding for projects came from a combination of public and private investment. National Lottery funding has had a considerable impact, along with financial aid from the European Regional Development Fund and the Central Manchester Development Corporation. English Heritage and English Partnerships have also helped to sustain and invest in the city's future and public realm.

The guide, divided into eight distinct but interrelated sections, covers a combination of interior projects in existing buildings and new build.

Together, these projects document and characterise Manchester's changing values and identity, from the decline in manufacturing to the rapid rise of service industries.

Fully to understand and appreciate the city's architecture, it may be useful to look at some of the key areas of Manchester that have shaped and determined its development.

Originally a Roman settlement, Castlefield was arguably the birthplace of Manchester. Around the mid-nineteenth century it witnessed the largest growth in its history, largely due to the industrial revolution. The rivers Medlock and Irwell were integral to its development, allowing goods to be brought in from the port of Liverpool and stored in warehouses in the basin. In 1877 the Cheshire Lines Company erected the massive Southern Iron Viaduct, still a prominent feature of the area. The combination of railway viaducts and canals has forged a distinct identity for the basin, now taken forward by new developments and refurbishments.

Eastgate Offices (see page 1.8), designed by Stephenson Bell, was perhaps the development that kick-started the area's regeneration in 1992. Jim Ramsbottom, a local property developer, began purchasing disused buildings in Castlefield to redevelop. The policy of his company, Castlefield Estates, is to avoid pastiche but maintain a clear distinction between the old and new (a good example is Ian Simpson's Merchants Warehouse, see page 1.12).

The only new building in Castlefield featured in this guide is Stephenson Bell's acclaimed and ultra-modern Quay Bar (see page 1.2). Though totally contrasting with its environment, its form was detemined by abstracting the layers and axes of its surrounding urban context. Similarly, the railway viaducts that criss-cross the area provided an excellent opportunity for the design of two new bars into the arches below. Barça (see page 1.18), co-owned by Hale Leisure and Mick Hucknall, is a post-industrial hard-edged venue, offering cool and cosmopolitanism with a distinct European flavour, reflected in its Barcelona-inspired name. The second, Nowhere bar, announces its presence from beneath the busy railway lines linking Manchester to the south.

The Northern Quarter on the opposite side of the city centre is comparable to Castlefield, originally home to numerous textile and cotton mills and renowned for its unique and gritty character. Following the opening of Affleck and Brown in 1901 (Manchester's famous 'Harrods of the North'), the Northern Quarter was regarded as the city's prime shopping district. When the Arndale Centre opened in 1976, however, the Northern Quarter was marginalised; it is now considered the creative quarter of the city and the incubator for the cultural industries. It provides a perfect meeting point between music and culture, offering an assortment of alternative retail outlets including sex shops, record outlets and trendy bars, giving the Northern Quarter a distinct community spirit unrivalled anywhere else in the city. Although the redevelopment of the Affleck and Brown department store into lofts (see page xx) has partially gentrified the district (as well as providing much-needed living space in the city centre), the Northern Quarter has kept its identity as a counter-cultural enclave and will continue to do so.

One notable local community-led organisation is the Northern Quarter Association (see page 6.6), whose main aim is to promote the area, while fighting to keep the integrity of the district intact. The work of two of its active members – Michael Trainer, co-founder of the association, and Dominic Sagar, local architect – is featured in the guide.

The Hulme area – home to thousands of workers in the mid- to late-nineteenth century, mostly crammed into slum dwellings – provides fine exemplars of new approaches to urban planning and regeneration. By the early 1920s, the average density of Manchester was 34 residents per acre, but Hulme, notorious for its squalor, had a staggering 136. Following World War 2, the council embarked on a clearance programme. In the late 1960s Stretford Road, the main arterial route through the area, was closed, precipitating the demise of numerous small shops and businesses.

With these massive changes occurring over a relatively short period, strong family networks and the community of Hulme were broken up and the people were dispersed throughout the region. During this time the district witnessed the arrival of the four huge crescent blocks that blighted the landscape for the next 20 years, housing 12,000 people where more than 130,000 people had once lived. After ten years of dissatisfaction, and numerous cases of poor health associated with sub-standard living conditions, Manchester City Council began to move people out of the blocks.

The Hulme City Challenge initiative, a £37.5 million government regeneration package, began in April 1992. Hulme's urban plan aimed to repair the damage of post-war and 1960s housing follies and knit together the urban fabric after disastrous segregation and zoning mistakes. It was largely implemented by two local urban-design and architectural advisors, Berridge Lowenburg & Greenberg and Mills Beaumont Leavey Channon (MBLC), whose work is featured in this guide.

Landmark projects in Hulme signify a new era in its development: the Hulme Arch bridge by Chris Wilkinson (see page 4.14), a symbolic gateway, is recognised nationally for its stunning contribution to architecture and engineering; MBLC's celebrated Homes for Change (see page

4.10) is a successful attempt to provide mixed-use housing with a strong emphasis on durability and sustainability; OMI's Boundary Lane scheme (see page 4.12), well received by residents and planners alike, tackles the issue of reintegration. On a smaller but no less important scale, Hodder Associates' 204 City Road surgery (see page 4.2) offers a patient-centred approach to design, on a tight budget. These schemes (among many others) are a welcome contribution to the process of renewal in a fractured urban community.

The docklands area of Manchester, notably Salford Quays, is also undergoing radical change: in the early 1980s the docks became redundant, mostly as a consequence of new forms of employment and recession. Dockland cranes were demolished and vast tracts of the port disappeared. Renewal, of a sort, followed. Large postmodern developments and offices emerged to accommodate the Thatcherite consciousness of the 1980s. More recently, Trafford and Salford City Councils' concern for mixed-use developments and sustainability have lead to a rich mixture of projects to reshape the area's future.

Michael Wilford's The Lowry (see page 7.6) is the first Quays flagship project, providing a base for the paintings of Salford's L S Lowry (1887–1976). The Imperial War Museum (North) by Daniel Libeskind (see page 7.4) will be situated opposite the Lowry Centre, aiming to attract a further 400,000 visitors to the area. Its 'shattered globe' form will be a dramatic metaphor for global conflict. Both will revive interest in the basin.

Adjacent to Salford Quays, Trafford Park is one of Europe's largest industrial estates. Created in 1894, it housed many well-known companies including Kellogg's, Metropolitan-Vickers and GEC. The Manchester United ground (see page 8.2) is currently situated there, its dramatic new stand dominating the Stretford skyline. Manchester City's ground in

Moss Side will be moving to the Commonwealth Stadium in Eastlands (see page 6.10) after the Commonwealth Games in 2002. Football aside, the £600 million Trafford Centre in Dumplington, heavily criticised for its 'cut-and-paste' architecture, presents themed shopping on a grotesque scale.

Another major factor in Manchester's diversity is its large student population. Manchester Metropolitan University has made a significant contribution to the city, providing high-quality education and enlightened architectural patronage. Notable are the new Hollins library; the Aytoun Street library and resource centre (designed by MBLC); and the Sir Geoffrey Manton building (see pages 3.6, 2.16, and 3.14, respectively). Buildings of this calibre will continue to attract students internationally, significantly adding to the city's cosmopolitan status.

Manchester also enjoys many buildings dating back to the industrial revolution and its associated wealth. The Reform Club on King Street (see page 2.42), originally home to the Liberal Party and nineteenth-century radicalism, has been refurbished in a highly decadent manner as a restaurant and bar. The Royal Exchange on St Anne's Square, once the centre of trading and commerce, now hosts the renovated Royal Exchange Theatre (see page 2.40).

Following the IRA bomb blast in the city centre, the need for a strategic repair plan to unify the disparate elements of the city was clear. EDAW's masterplan included reinstating the Royal Exchange; refurbishing the Corn Exchange; creating a 'Millennium Quarter' encompassing the cathedral; and building the largest Marks and Spencer's store in Europe. The Bridgewater Hall by RHWL (see page 2.64), home to the Hallé Orchestra, establishes a permanent base for classical music, broadening Manchester's international profile and making a strong statement about

Manchester: a guide to recent architecture

the city's cultural aspirations. Calatrava's Trinity Bridge (see page 2.54) across the River Irwell joins the cities of Salford and Manchester, and provides a symbol of the regeneration of the Chapel Wharf area.

This massive reappraisal of the city centre and progressive redevelopment agenda is a brave and ambitious attempt to redefine the future of a city in motion.

ACKNOWLEDGEMENTS

This book is dedicated to Alice Gittins and Emily Parker.

David Hands would like to thank the following people who have provided support and encouragement throughout the duration of writing this book, in particular; Sarah Chandler for her help at the initial stages of the project; Kevin Singh, at UCE for his much needed support and incisive advice; Patrick Hannay, Mike Fleetwood and Howard Harris at UWIC, Cardiff who have enabled me to get this far; Joanne Green, Ruth Lee, Lucy Ashton, Camelia G S Paton and Vicky Avery Gee for their comments and generosity of ideas, and especially my long suffering flatmate Ruth Dillon for her great understanding; last but by no means least, I would like to extend my gratidute to my family for their patience and encouragement over the last year.

Sarah Parker would like to thank Jay, Nick, Alywyn, Robin and Hugh for their helpful encouragement and involvement in this project; Tony Crabbe, Brynn Taylor, and Karen Bull from NTU for their belief; personal thanks to family and friends for their endurance and finally a big thank you to Glenys Shellard, Paul Knowles and Jerry Pitman at Siemens for their patience and support.

We would both like to thank Tom Neville for allowing us the indulgence to write this guide; to Professor Bob Jerrard; and a big thank you to all the architects and designers that have taken part in this project.
DH and SP

Using this guide

The guide is divided into eight sections, each based around an area of Manchester with its own character and buildings of interest. Greater Manchester covers an area of 500 square miles. Manchester proper is a compact city, with a population of around 438,000. When the whole of Greater Manchester is included, the population rises to 3 million, making the city the second largest in England.

Most of the projects in central Manchester can be reached on foot, and a Manchester A-Z *Street Atlas* is recommended for visitors unfamiliar with the city – A-Z map co-ordinates for each entry are listed with the address at the bottom of the page. Maps are usually inexpensive, but always invaluable and can be purchased from any bookshop. For further information about a specific area, visit the Tourist Information Centre next to the central library in St Peter's Square.

Public transport is frequent and moderately priced; the new Metrolink system has made a considerable improvement. Tickets for the Metrolink have to be purchased prior to the journey and are valid for one day's travel. Taxis are easy to find, and black cabs are recommended for comfort and competitive prices. A fast, cheap rail link from Manchester Airport 8 miles south of the city connects both terminals to Piccadilly mainline train station in the centre. Services are frequent and generally reliable.

A motorway link runs from the airport joining the M56, providing direct access to the wider region. The M60 is Manchester's orbital route, similar to the M25 circling London.

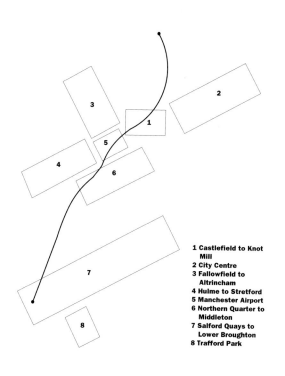

1 Castlefield to Knot Mill
2 City Centre
3 Fallowfield to Altrincham
4 Hulme to Stretford
5 Manchester Airport
6 Northern Quarter to Middleton
7 Salford Quays to Lower Broughton
8 Trafford Park

Castlefield to Knott Mill

Quay Bar

The Quay Bar, one of many fashionable bars in the Castlefield Basin, is situated on the edge of the Bridgewater Canal. The client, Wolverhampton and Dudley Breweries (better known for Banks's traditional pubs), wanted a contemporary solution that would provide both living space for the bar manager and a dining/bar space.

The form of the bar was determined by abstracting the layers and axes of the surrounding urban context: the busy Chester Road that sits on top of the Bridgewater viaduct; the Bridgewater canal; and a 3-metre-wide tunnel (built by the Duke of Bridgewater's engineers to divert the River Medlock) that runs beneath the site. Constructed in three levels, the building slots into this landscape as it descends from the Chester Road to the canalside 4.5 metres below, creating a dialogue between private and public space. The upper storeys take the form of a white 'living stack', a modernist box clearly influenced by the 1930s international style, containing two apartments stacked one on top of the other. Its stainless-steel-seamed stair tower, aquamarine glass light shaft and white render contrast with the robust Victorian context of the area. The combination of these elements also makes reference to the beacon of the Eastgate building on the other side of the canal basin, by the same architect.

As the lower levels of the building are not visible from Chester Road, entering the bar is like entering a Tardis. Tight and formal in plan at the top, the opening up of the building to the canalside is an unexpected pleasure. This unfolding was informed by the parallels of the Chester Road which, as the architect Roger Stephenson said, 'reverberate through the site', defining each level until they break down at the waterfront. Seduced by the spirit of 'new modernism', you are lead into the building at viaduct level over a footbridge on to the mezzanine. This entrance is edged by patinated copper panelling that continues inside. The strong

Stephenson Bell 1998

Stephenson Bell 1998

Quay Bar

parallel lines are broken down by vast double-height terne-coated stainless-steel fins, slicing the interior at diagonals. The fins form junctions with the heavy-duty doors leading to the timber-deck broadwalk on the canalside. On the mezzanine level the canalside can also be reached via the roof terrace and splayed stair that follows the axes of the tunnel beneath the site.

Internally, there is a strong emphasis on the horizontal to highlight the parallel planes defining each level: the red brick of the back of bar and mezzanine walls which adds warmth to the light and airy space; the steel balustrading to the mezzanine edge; and the detailing on the multi-ply toilet doors, bars, stainless-steel fins, glazing and timber decking of the broadwalk. These all contrast with the vertical emphasis of stainless steel stair tower and vertical scale of internal space.

As the building contrasts totally with its context, it is a successful antithesis to its competitors – all red-brick Victorian structures. The only disappointment is the quality of the workmanship in some areas, especially on the stainless-steel fins. Quay could also benefit from designing new menus to complement the bar's form, a complex and modern interpretation of the surrounding layered environs.

ADDRESS Deansgate Quay, Bridgewater Viaduct, Castlefield, Manchester [6c 94]
CLIENT Wolverhampton and Dudley Brewery
STRUCTURAL ENGINEER Stuart and Harris
CONTRACT VALUE £1.4 million
METROLINK G-MEX
ACCESS open

Stephenson Bell 1998

Stephenson Bell 1998

Nowhere Bar

The Nowhere Bar exhibits a high degree of 'spatial gymnastics', beneath and beyond the existing railway viaduct, emerging as if from nowhere. Fronting on to busy Deansgate and best appreciated from the Metrolink line opposite, the bar projects a striking presence.

Arranged on ground and mezzanine levels, the quality of the interior is fully appreciated as the user travels through its contrasting aspects. A wall of glazed screens protrudes from the arches on the Castle Street elevation, creating a dramatic entrance to the bar area.

The central bar is situated deep within the building, linking the Deansgate side of Nowhere to the main entrance area, acting as a nodal point, drawing drinkers into the lounge. An enclosed staircase provides access to the mezzanine and funnels patrons into a more relaxed drinking area. Weather permitting, people can enjoy their drinks on the flat roof adjoining the mezzanine. A lightweight curved canopy provides cover on the Castle Street balcony with views on to the street and canal, and seating and tables are arranged on its perimeter.

Nowhere Bar is a masterly display of space planning – an imaginative approach to a highly constrained site. Though some aspects of detailing and finishes could be more fully resolved (notably the gold paintwork on exposed steelwork), Nowhere has quite evidently succeeded.

ADDRESS 374 Deansgate, Manchester [5C 94]
CLIENT In-House Leisure Limited
STRUCTURAL ENGINEER Blackwood Structural Design (Manchester)
CONTRACT VALUE £350,000
METROLINK GMEX
ACCESS check opening hours

Judge Gill Associates 1996

Judge Gill Associates 1996

Eastgate Offices

Entrepreneur and former bookie Jim Ramsbottom of Castlefield Estates saw Castlefield's potential in the 1980s and bought five out of seven buildings on the site. He bought the Eastgate building when it reached the end of its life as a ragmop factory. The area was developed in stages, with each building benefiting from grant assistance from the Central Manchester Development Corporation. Eastgate Offices was the second structure to be refurbished after the bar Dukes 92, in what used to be a stable building. These two established the development philosophy for the area: to preserve each building's structural and historical integrity.

The brief was to provide studio and office space for Manchester's creative and new-media community, an idea from development consultant Nick Johnson. This was a courageous move in the economic climate of the time but in spite of the recession the majority of the building was let on completion in 1992.

Surrounded by water on three sides, the building is situated on a large peninsular and is the first to be reached by road from Castle Street, a link to the rest of the city. The rear of the building runs parallel to the Rochdale Canal to the north, overlooking the viaducts that dissect the area; the south and east sides face the curve of the Bridgewater Canal. The footprint is in the form of a giant knife, the triangular tip of its blade punctuated by horizontal glazing panels which enclose an escape stairway.

Externally, the pattern of the original façade has been enlivened by two new insertions. The most expressive and fundamental of these is the new entrance which projects outwards, announcing the building to the street. Tracing the eastern wall of Agricola's Roman fort, its primary wall slices diagonally through the façade, eventually dissolving inside the reception area. The existing water tower (which was badly damaged) has been modernised to house a stair-and-lift core with services at its top. This

Stephenson Bell 1992

Castlefield to Knott Mill

Stephenson Bell 1992

Eastgate Offices

forms a beacon that glows aquamarine at night, with glazing resembling a channel-set gem.

Internally, the purity of the white-painted plasterboard gives way to the building's traditional features, the most impressive being the exposed roof structure on the top floor, best viewed from the new mezzanine. The use of new materials coheres with those existing, while adding a crispness to the fabric of the warehouse. Volumes have been opened up in places, especially in the double-height café overlooking the Rochdale Canal. The building's widths and depths made it ideal for flexible office conversion; overall, this has resulted in tenants who enjoy occupying a comfortable and light working environment with more personality than an anonymous suspended-ceiling office block.

The architects have created a building with a 'contextual modernism' (a term lightheartedly coined by Stephenson) which neither ignores the past nor parodies of it.

ADDRESS Eastgate, Castle Street, Castlefield, Manchester [5C 94]
CLIENT Mark Addy Limited (Jim Ramsbottom)
STRUCTURAL ENGINEER Buro Happold
SIZE 3114 square metres
CONTRACT VALUE £1.75 million (tender price)
METROLINK GMEX
BUS 69, 84, 230, 252, 258, 264 to Deansgate
ACCESS by appointment

Stephenson Bell 1992

Stephenson Bell 1992

Merchants Warehouse

The Merchants Warehouse, built in 1827 early in the industrial revolution, is the oldest warehouse in Castlefield and was the third of Jim Ramsbottom's buildings to be redeveloped (see page 1.8). Ramsbottom bought the building, now grade-2 listed, at its derelict value of £25,000 and wanted to develop it as a flagship project. Having a track record in contemporary regeneration projects in Knott Mill, where they restored their offices, Ian Simpson Architects, who were also instrumental in developing a design strategy for the area, were commissioned after winning a competition.

The first priority was to make the building structurally sound and weathertight, an extensive job as the warehouse is four storey on the canal side and three on the street side, and was in a state of dereliction. Using reclaimed brick and timber, the architects had to rebuild the north gable destroyed by fire in 1981 and build a new roof to repair bomb damage from World War 2.

The scheme's most prominent elements are two glass bookends on each gable end, reinforcing the building's flagship status. These are supported by sandstone walls (a reference to the sandstone bedrock in the canal basin) and function as self-contained stair and service cores, providing the building's main circulation. They also maximise lettable space, an important consideration for speculative office development.

Split longitudinally into six bays, the building is penetrated by two canal arms on either side of a full-height central crosswall. These were once centres of activity where goods were unloaded from barges and winched upwards to be distributed on each side of the warehouse. The architects have restored and refitted the building by emphasising these features.

Each bay is characterised by a loophole with arched windows on either

Ian Simpson Architects 1994

Merchants Warehouse

Ian Simpson Architects 1994

side, double-glazed with window frames designed to be in keeping with the existing building. To maximise light penetration, circulation and floor space, the architects opened up the warehouse as much as possible: crosswalls were cut back 3 metres from the external wall; an openable rooflight was inserted; and rectangular slots were cut in the floor allowing light to enter 20 metres into the building. These slots also enable a framed view of the impressive loft space that contains the warehouse's old winding gear. Sadly the tenant's fit-out consultant (appointed after Simpson) filled in the light slots at first- and second-floor levels, due to the need for confidentiality. The two arches of the canal arms penetrating the building are elegantly glazed with a structural glass wall, again to flood the building with light. Like the light slots in the floor, the aperture through these arches has been blocked by partitions that do not follow the concept of the original fit-out, proportionally or aesthetically.

Overall the new additions complement rather than compete with the existing structure but it's a shame that the dialogue between the architects and fit-out consultants was not clear enough to preserve the detail of the original scheme. Symptomatic of commercial development, all the architect can do is ensure that promotional photographs are taken before the tenant moves in.

ADDRESS Castlefield, Manchester [5C 94]
CLIENT Castlefield Estates (Jim Ramsbottom)
STRUCTURAL ENGINEER SMP/Atelier One – Phase 1
CONTRACT VALUE £2.6 million
METROLINK G-MEX
BUS 69, 84, 230, 252, 258, 264 to Deansgate
ACCESS limited

Ian Simpson Architects 1994

Merchants Warehouse

Ian Simpson Architects 1994

Castlefield Footbridge

This small and unassuming footbridge is a direct response to its context: it is clad with Locharbriggs sandstone to harmonise with the surrounding warehouse buildings and to refer to the bedrock of the canal basin. Like other projects in the area it was grant assisted by the Central Manchester Development Corporation.

Passing over the Rochdale Canal, the bridge, 15 metres in length and held in tension by a stainless-steel radiused frame, links the derelict northside with the heart of the Castlefield Basin. This is reached through a passage between the Eastgate Offices by Stephenson Bell (see page 1.8) and the Bass Warehouse (another Ramsbottom building) recently refurbished by OMI Architects.

Fourteen 1200 x 1200 x 175 mm stone blocks with curved tops doubling as handrails form each side of the bridge, slotting between stainless-steel uprights that are welded to the frame. The deck was constructed in layers and is composed of granite sets laid on red in-situ concrete, poured on to reinforcing mesh. The frame is supported at each end by stainless-steel shoes resting on stone-clad abutments.

Seamless and elegant, a simple formula and a rational approach has resulted in a bridge that is far more honest than the cast-iron version originally suggested by the client.

ADDRESS Rochdale Canal, Castlefield, Manchester [5C 94]
CLIENT Castlefield Estates
STRUCTURAL ENGINEER Modus
CONTRACT VALUE £140,000
METROLINK GMEX
BUS 69, 84, 230, 252, 258, 264 to Deansgate
ACCESS open

Ian Simpson Architects 1998

Castlefield Footbridge

Castlefield to Knott Mill

Ian Simpson Architects 1998

Barça

Barça occupies two adjacent railway arches at the heart of Castlefield Basin, marking the junction with the Southern Iron Viaduct that towers overhead. Built in 1877 by the Cheshire Lines Company, the viaduct's monumental scale is felt throughout the area, dividing the canal network to the north from Catalan Square to the south.

Barça is the third regeneration project in the area, the result of a joint venture between Hale Leisure (who owned the arches and with whom Harrison Ince had a track record) and So What Arts (who manage the band Simply Red). The clients wanted a solution that would stand out within the sturdy industrial context of the area. Harrison Ince have designed a tapas bar inspired by the surrounding historical structures but with a distinctly Spanish flavour ('Barça' derives from 'Barcelona' and continues the Spanish theme in the square).

A loadbearing sandstone spine wall marks the route from north to south as it dissects the arches from the canal basin to Catalan Square, forming a dynamic relationship with the front and back of the building. On the north elevation, the composition of elements looks like an elaborate post-industrial stage set. This is dominated by a new insertion projecting out of an arch at 90 degrees to the spine wall. Illuminated at night, a partially ruined existing wall adds to the theatrical effect. A mixture of glass block and clear glazing slices through and fills in the existing structures, providing views across the canal basin.

The south face of the building opens out on to Catalan Square. Directly under the arches, the first floor nestles under a brick-vaulted ceiling. Its balcony, punctuated by a timber-and-steel stair to pavement level, provides extra space for diners and those attending private functions. The balcony is sheltered by a curved steel roof that follows the line of the railway arch.

Harrison Ince 1996

Harrison Ince 1996

Barça

Internally, the architects have created an adventure playground of differing levels, surfaces and voids that allow both intimate and public spaces. This layering is further expressed by the rich use of materials, both contemporary and traditional, from a raised existing pitch-pine floor in the centre of the bar area, to the stone floor at the entrance perimeter. Stainless steel and glass blocks are used to help diffuse and reflect a mixture of natural and artificial light, softening the hard-edged post-industrial aesthetic.

This was a risky project from the outset; the imagination of the architects, foresight of the developers and association with 'Mr Simply Red' have resulted in one of the most fashionable bars in Manchester.

ADDRESS Catalan Square, Castlefield, Manchester [5C 94]
CLIENT Newlight Limited
STRUCTURAL ENGINEER Blackwood Structural Design
CONTRACT VALUE £700,000
METROLINK G-MEX
BUS 69, 84, 230, 252, 258, 264 to Deansgate
ACCESS open

Harrison Ince 1996

Harrison Ince 1996

Merchants' Bridge

Situated in Castlefield Basin, Merchants' Bridge spans the Bridgewater Canal at its junction with the Rochdale Canal. With a strong resonance of its nineteenth-century glory as a vibrant industrial area, Castlefield Basin demanded a bridge unique in character which also respected its traditional context.

The steel footbridge, spanning a distance of 40 metres, features a curvaceous single arch that delicately counterbalances the 3-metre-wide curved deck, allowing the deck to remain in a state of perfect equilibrium. Thirteen inclined tapered hangers link the deck to the arch, while not detracting from its slender appearance. Sensitive use of lighting accentuates its sculptural qualities after dark, making the bridge a focal point in the canal basin.

Access to Merchants' Bridge is gained from two particular points, but the easiest and the best is via the front of Barça café-bar (see page 1.18). The designers unashamedly acknowledge Santiago Calatrava as a major influence in their approach to the overall design, placing great emphasis on the use of torsion.

The best vantage point for fully appreciating Merchants' Bridge is gained from high above on the Altrincham to Manchester Metrolink line.

ADDRESS Castlefield Basin, Manchester [5C 94]
CONSULTANT ARCHITECT RHWL
OWNER AND DEVELOPER Central Manchester Development Corporation
CONTRACTOR P Casey (Civil Engineering)
METROLINK G-MEX
BUS 69, 84, 230, 252, 258, 264 to Deansgate
ACCESS open

Whitby Bird & Partners 1994

Whitby Bird & Partners 1994

Antony H Wilson Apartment

Antony Wilson is a much-respected figure in the northwest of England, best remembered as a presenter on Granada TV and founding father of Factory Records. Ben Kelly helped shape Factory Record's image, designing the Haçienda in 1982 and Dry 201 in 1989, as well as the company's headquarters in Charles Street. Since the demise of Factory Records, closure of the Haçienda, and change of ownership of Dry 201, Wilson's apartment is the only physical reminder of the empire.

The apartment is located in Knott Mill, among Manchester's community of design-led architects, including Ian Simpson Architects who were primarily responsible for the building's overall renovation, assisted by a City of Manchester Development Corporation grant.

The central space of the apartment was kept open with functional elements of the interior pushed to the periphery. The room revolves around a massive, centrally placed worktable, designed by Kelly and constructed within the room itself. The kitchen area is partly concealed by a plywood storage unit that also acts as a screen. Glazed coloured tiling surrounds the kitchen walls, echoing the Haçienda's industrial aesthetic. Some of the most ingenious and finely detailed elements are featured in the bathroom, complemented by the use of industrial scaffolding tubes as towel rails and shelving. A delightful intimate office space is located above the main living area, linked by a reclaimed steel staircase fixed diagonally. Reclaimed oak flooring provides warmth and unity and also offers an excellent means to conceal cabling running underneath.

ADDRESS Little Peter Street, Knott Mill, Manchester [6C 94]
METROLINK G-MEX
BUS 69, 84, 230, 252, 258, 264 to Deansgate
ACCESS none

Ben Kelly Design 1998

Antony H Wilson Apartment

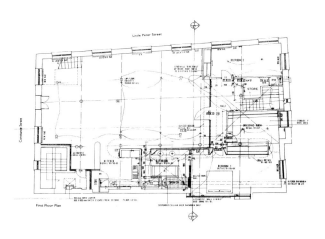

First Floor Plan

Ben Kelly Design 1998

Castlefield to Knott Mill

City Centre

Malmaison

Comfort, affordability and style capture the essence and marketing manifesto of the Malmaison hotels, created by hotelier Ken McCulloch and interior designer Amanda Rosa. The chain offers a competitively priced design-led alternative to the 1970s brutality of Manchester's Piccadilly Hotel owned by the corporate giant Jarvis Hotels.

Developed using a consortium of talents – the shell designed by Darby Associates and the interior by Amanda Rosa – the hotel is a partnership between the old and the new. Its 112 rooms accommodate an existing Victorian building, a former warehouse for textile manufacturers Joshua Hoyles, with a new extension sited on what was the Imperial Hotel. This was allegedly home to Manchester United players in the early 1900s, an association that has been parodied in the red, white and black colours of the reception area.

The architects wanted the extension to contrast boldly with the ornate and articulate detailing of the existing building. To avoid pastiche the new façade is grey-granite aggregate and concrete block. Designed to be sinister and secretive, its bulky, aggressive form rests surprisingly easily behind the Hoyles building, sliding into a former lightwell in its v-shaped plan. This juxtaposition has informally bonded the two volumes, creating a large hard-landscaped piazza, clearly identifying the hotel's presence and purpose, only minutes from Piccadilly Station.

As well as providing a car drop-off point, and noise protection for the rooms, the piazza emphasises the main hotel entrance, a focal point reinforced by a huge flying glazed canopy. Inspired by the canopies of the Paris Métro, this dramatically engages the old with the new. A dedicated entrance has also been provided for the brasserie, designed to sustain itself and bring new custom to the hotel, and *vice versa*. The 'Mal' is a dining experience in its own right.

Darby Associates 1998

Malmaison

City Centre

Darby Associates 1998

Malmaison

The main vertical circulation route is located in the new building and is enclosed behind the curved wall of the façade. Lit at night, its Reglit glazing provides ghostly silhouettes of the pedestrian movement within.

The exterior deliberately bears little resemblance to the interior, which from the dark and intimate detailing of the brasserie to the very derivative signage takes art deco as its main inspiration. This is not the only reference to French chic: Malmaison takes its name from the Chateau Malmaison, home of Empress Josephine and Napoleon, and the furniture and striped fabrics in the sumptuous interior echo the Empire style.

The hotel rooms vary in size – more spacious in the existing building, smaller in the new – with bold colours, deco prints and custom-designed soft furnishings lending a sophisticated and relaxed atmosphere. The only references to context are black and white photographs of local architecture, a theme repeated throughout all the hotels.

Labelled 'a temple of hotel chic' by *The Economist*, the success of this chain must be applauded. The architect's pragmatic approach confidently announces Malmaison to Manchester, though the quality of the external detailing does not quite match up to the elegance of the interior.

ADDRESS London Road, Piccadilly, Manchester [5F 95]
CLIENT Malmaison Limited
STRUCTURAL ENGINEER Shephard Gilmour and Partners
METROLINK Piccadilly
BUS 192, 196, 200–207, 395
ACCESS open

Darby Associates 1998

Malmaison

City Centre

Darby Associates 1998

Communiqué Offices

Communiqué is an established PR company based in the bustling Canal Street area. The office refurbishment was integral to the company's drive to raise its market profile and provide a dynamic working environment.

The architect has completely reworked the existing space in this four-storey warehouse building. The main focus of the scheme is the stairway linking all floors, providing dramatic viewpoints throughout the interior. A large spine wall divides the open-plan office in two, clearly separating public and private spaces. Large areas of flooring have been stripped back to reveal the steelwork of the original structure. The addition of conference rooms was a subtle and ingenious move – set back from the front façade, and linked to the main office space.

Traditional industrial materials have been sandblasted and cleaned to reinvigorate their former robust qualities, complemented by pitch-pine timber and a bold use of colour. All the new insertions have their own distinct language and are instantly distinguishable from the existing structure, with the building's history echoing with its new use.

The offices are an excellent example of their type, providing an elegant yet robust environment for the occupants.

ADDRESS 2 Canal Street, Manchester [5E 95]
CLIENT Communiqué PR Ltd
STRUCTURAL ENGINEER Blackwood Structural Design
CONTRACT VALUE £200,000
METROLINK Piccadilly Gardens
BUS 11, 16, 42, 109, 126, 143, 157
ACCESS lobby only

Harrison Ince 1996

Harrison Ince 1996

Mash and Air

Austin Powers meets Barbarella in this funky neo-pop interior designed by Marc Newson. The overall concept for the bar/restaurant was the brainchild of Oliver Peyton, an entrepreneurial restaurateur. Peyton's other adventures include London's fashionable eatery Coast whose interior, also designed by Newson, expresses a contemporary simulation of 1960s futurism.

On entering Mash and Air from Chorlton Street in Manchester's 'gay village', you are assaulted by an overwhelming rush of lime green covering every seamless and uninterrupted surface, from the floor to the suspended ceiling which is punctured by recessed opaque circular lights.

The bar and restaurant are split into distinct but related areas, 'Mash' and 'Air'. Each of them conveys a different atmosphere, but they share the same curvy theme. Mash (the name of a stage in the brewing process) occupies two floors of drinking and eating space with the entire design focused around a day-glo-orange micro-brewery. The brewing equipment's white cylindrical volume is the building's main organising element and it can be seen through portholes. On the first floor the lime-green bar curves around this focal point which is lined with stools upholstered in electric blue to match the fabric on the chunky-curvy purpose-designed furniture elsewhere. Air, the restaurant and private dining room, occupies the top floor, which is painted pale blue.

Every detail has a playful and fluid form which is very much an obsession of Newson's, and is perhaps more famously associated with his industrial design, from the neoprene Embryo Chair for Cappellini to a modular retail system for fashion label W&LT. Indeed, the tap-like form of the door handles in Mash strongly evoke the spirit of Alessi, another of Newson's clients.

Limited by the budget, Mash and Air is not as well finished or as high

Marc Newson with Harrison Ince 1996

Marc Newson with Harrison Ince 1996

Mash and Air

profile as Newson's other projects. Though created for a mixed clientele, Mash and Air's boldness and subtly camp nature works well in its context, and proves that Newson (whose original training was in jewellery design) can direct his highly innovative talent to any design brief.

ADDRESS 40 Chorlton Street, Manchester [4E 95]
Client Oliver Peyton
SIZE 12,000 square feet
METROLINK Mosley Street or Piccadilly
BUS 11, 16, 42, 109, 126, 143, 157
ACCESS open

Marc Newson with Harrison Ince 1996

Marc Newson with Harrison Ince 1996

Northwest Film Archive

This delightful addition to the entrance lobby to the Northwest Film Archive, easy to overlook due to its quiet and unassuming location, is just off Minshull Street in Minshull House. The original building is a grade-2 listed 1840s wharfside granary, previously home to the Manchester Metropolitan University's library. Owing to its relocation to the new Aytoun Street building (designed by the same architect, see page 2.16) there was considerable floor space vacant within the building. This provided an excellent opportunity to expand the archive.

Its restrained box-entrance – with clear glazing projecting a formal (but inviting) image to visitors – acts as a direct reference point to an otherwise largely anonymous building, ensuring unhindered access to the archive. This is also assisted by a paved ramp catering for wheelchair users.

An *in-situ* concrete wall penetrates into the lobby, supporting the light steel-framed roof and successfully breaking down the divisions between the interior and exterior spaces. Two more external walls add support, enclosing the circular door below, reducing the entrance structure to a minimum.

It succinctly highlights the architects' approach to detailing: elegance through simplicity combined with a sense of delight in the juxtaposition of new and old. Well worth a visit, though hard to find.

ADDRESS Minshull Street, Manchester [4E 95]
CLIENT Northwest Film Archive
SIZE 520 square metres
CONTRACT VALUE £620,000
METROLINK Piccadilly
BUS 11, 16, 42, 109, 126, 143, 157
ACCESS check prior to visiting

Mills Beaumont Leavey Channon 1997

Mills Beaumont Leavey Channon 1997

Prague Five

Prague Five is a popular place to be seen – day or night, gay or straight, it's a place to eat and drink, with music encompassing dance sounds and the blues.

The original character of the interior has been allowed to speak for itself, with minimum intervention from the architects. The basement is exposed brickwork, apart from a wall above the raised dance platform that has been painted electric blue and sprinkled with gold stars. The bar is supported by a glass-block wall that is back-lit to cast out icy blue light, barely reflected in the hard stone floor. Furniture is designed for transience rather than comfort, with rectangular and circular tables resembling those of the picnic-bench and pub-garden variety.

In comparison to the gothic space of the basement, the restaurant area on the ground floor is slightly more refined. Nestling under the brick-vaulted roof, high-back chairs (with stars punched out of their metal surface) and calm timber flooring add to the convivial atmosphere.

Stripped to the bare minimum, this is an almost timeless industrial aesthetic. Unlike some of the more stylised bars, Prague Five has the potential to transform itself to suit the appetite of the passing crowd.

ADDRESS Canal Street, Manchester [5E 95]
CLIENT Hale Leisure
METROLINK Piccadilly Gardens
BUS 11, 16, 42, 109, 126, 143, 157
ACCESS open

Harrison Ince 1993

Harrison Ince 1993

Aytoun Street Library

When the lease expired on their library in Minshull Street, Manchester Metropolitan University decided to build a new Learning Resource Centre (LRC) in the city centre. With the critical acclaim of the recently completed Siemens building, the university approached the architects to design them a 'statement' building in the same expression as Siemens'.

The central location of the Aytoun Street library was chosen to allow easy access for users. Bordered by UMIST, Sheena Simon College and the gay village, the building is at a busy intersection of traffic routes, highlighting the university's prominent position as one of the leading academic institutions in Manchester, while also providing a powerful focal point for the area.

A tight 14-month schedule for the LRC's design and construction combined with unforeseen problems caused by a brook running 15 metres beneath the library presented the architects with considerable on-site difficulties. Sleek white aluminium rain-screen panels envelop the building's steel frame and concrete floors, with *brise-soleils* at third-floor level affording adequate protection from solar gain.

The library works on many levels of complexity, with transparency and its spatial configuration central to its success. The form of the building responds sensitively to the existing street pattern, curving gracefully around the contours of the site, while at the same time unifying the buildings of the main campus to the rear. A high degree of transparency provides the interior with an ethereal quality, allowing light to penetrate deep into the building, presenting the user with a relaxed and pleasant work environment.

In an attempt to prevent the theft of books from the library, all the windows are sealed, but the building does not seem to suffer from this potential drawback, with natural ventilation circulating in the majority

Mills Beaumont Leavey Channon 1993

Mills Beaumont Leavey Channon 1993

of the ground floor and comfort-cooled upper floors. When asked, the majority of its users considered the new library to be more conducive to concentration, and believed that the spacious atmosphere actually encouraged positive study.

ADDRESS Aytoun Street, Manchester [5F 95]
CLIENT Manchester Metropolitan University
STRUCTURAL ENGINEER YRM Anthony Hunt Associates
CONTRACT VALUE £4 million
SIZE 4018 square metres
METROLINK Piccadilly Gardens
BUS 11, 16, 42, 109, 126, 143, 157
ACCESS by appointment only

Mills Beaumont Leavey Channon 1993

Mills Beaumont Leavey Channon 1993

Manchester School of Management

Manchester is a city renowned for its large student population, with three universities co-existing within a mile of one another . The three collide at the junction of Booth Street and Oxford Road, creating a critical melting pot of academic cultures. The new building for the Manchester School of Management (MSM)is strategically placed to unify the three education schools, drawing on their diverse resources.

Predominantly clad in a robust Lazonby red sandstone, the MSM projects a gritty presence, in keeping with the Manchester vernacular. The building has been developed around a large central atrium, allowing daylight to penetrate throughout the school.

The two lower floors of the building house lecture theatres, seminar rooms and computer suites, each neatly inserted into the structural grid of the building, visible from both inside and out. Above, three floors are devoted to the heavily used office and teaching rooms. The central steel staircase allows unfettered movement through the space, providing users with a clear means of orientating themselves within the interior.

Internal finishes are hard wearing – minimising maintenance costs was a consideration the architect took fully into account. It is remarkable that a building of this quality was designed and built on a minuscule budget, proving yet again that good design need not be a costly indulgence.

ADDRESS Oxford Road, Manchester [1E 109]
CLIENT UMIST
STRUCTURAL AND M&E ENGINEER Ove Arup & Partners
CONTRACT VALUE £5 million
BUS 11, 17, 44, 47, 115, 130, 253
ACCESS none

ORMS 1998

ORMS 1998

Fourth Church of Christ the Scientist

Places of worship provide the ultimate challenge for architects: how to reinterpret the archetypal forms associated with various religious buildings while retaining their spiritual significance.

Historically, the Christian Scientists have had a reputation for being closed and secretive and this was reflected in their previous premises that turned its back on the street. The new church has upturned this ethos, and it now occupies the basement, ground and first floors of a former car showroom, a 1950s Portland stone building. Through careful manipulation of light, space and volume the architects have created a church that not only celebrates the Christian faith, but also promotes an open relationship with the public realm.

All public areas on the ground floor – the bookshop, reading room and main foyer – are arranged around a two-storey, 7.5-metre-high auditorium, at the heart of the church. Tight in plan and complex in spatial organisation, the composition of volumes and planes creates a series of apertures large enough to attract passers-by into the building. From the street, the interplay of the opaque and clear glass panes of the façade offers both transparency and privacy, with glimpses into the auditorium space.

The juxtaposition of a gallery with a viewing platform encourages engagement with the congregation. A folded steel-plate stair leading to ancillary spaces on the first floor is also visible from the street; its ascending journey appears to depict the rocky path to righteousness and enlightenment. This heavenly gesture is also reflected in the materiality and lighting: huge white planar walls in the auditorium are backlit with yellow lights that distribute a warm, soft glow in the gaps between the planes. Hard materials were employed at lower levels, such as the steel and glass of the main stair, which is softened at a higher level by timber handrails.

OMI Architects 1998

Fourth Church of Christ the Scientist

City Centre

OMI Architects 1998

Fourth Church of Christ the Scientist

Auditorium seating is in rich cherry wood, arranged in a semi-circular pattern around a beech dais, an informal arrangement encouraging both a participatory and performance-led service. The cross forms part of the structure above the dais.

Well thought-out and exquisitely detailed, a project with a difficult brief has resulted in a spiritually uplifting new church that possesses an architectural integrity on a par with David Chipperfield's First Church of Christ the Scientist.

ADDRESS 38–42 Peter Street, Manchester [5D 94]
CLIENT Seddon Developments
STRUCTURAL ENGINEER Modus Consulting Engineers
CONTRACT VALUE £500,000
SIZE 475 square metres
METROLINK St Peter's Square
BUS 11, 17, 44, 47, 115, 130, 253
ACCESS open

OMI Architects 1998

OMI Architects 1998

Fairburn Building, UMIST

Founded in 1824 by a group of industrialists, the University of Manchester, Institute of Science and Technology (UMIST) has a reputation for world-class innovation. In recent years its achievements have been rewarded by two Prince of Wales Awards for Innovation and the Queen's Award for Export Achievement, ranking it sixth in research institutions in the UK.

Named after Sir William Fairburn, distinguished scientist and an originator of the institute, the building is a conversion of two former cotton warehouses designed in 1896 by Charles Clegg and Sons. The need to repair each building's structural fabric, along with the spatial restructuring necessary for open-plan use presented the architects with a challenging but familiar brief. With a track record in warehouse conversion and a practice vocabulary of 'careful restoration coupled with contemporary expression', Stephenson Bell modernised the building while retaining as much of its original character as possible.

Although the two buildings are now integrated the existing entrances were retained. Access to a new public computer facility is through the doorway at No. 70, leading straight up to the first floor. No. 72's remodelled double-height foyer leads to three floors of offices with shared boardroom and conference facilities for the Estates Department and UMIST Ventures Limited.

A rectangle of planar elements in concrete, timber and brick creates a sense of intrigue and discovery, marking the doorway to the main circulation core to the office accommodation. The sense of direction is emphasised by a profile sheet-steel stair that runs up the back of the space, parallel to the street elevation, made visible as its metal edge cuts through the pitch-pine planar wall it scales behind. Glimpses of activity are also possible through a tall, skinny window that allows split-level views into

Stephenson Bell 1992

Stephenson Bell 1992

the workshop space on the upper ground level. Adding to the irony, a rusted steel I-beam rests sculpturally on a cast-iron column. This is complemented by a solitary winding mechanism, both objects standing as playful reminders of the building's past.

The new stair and glass-back lift that ascend up the front of the building give views over the city. The steel-and-concrete skeletal form of the new dogleg stair is bound on two sides by concrete walls; their detail echoes the architectural style of Tadao Ando.

Like much of this practice's work, the detailing of this project brings together past and present in diverse textures and finishes from simple steel handrails to exposed conduits and cable trays. These contrasts symbolise Manchester's gritty reinvention of modernism; in this case, the trait is not taken too seriously.

ADDRESS 70–72 Sackville Street, Manchester [5F 95]
CLIENT UMIST
STRUCTURAL ENGINEER Brian Clancy and Partners
CONTRACT VALUE £1.2 million
SIZE 2110 square metres
METROLINK Piccadilly
BUS 11, 17, 44, 47, 115, 130, 253
ACCESS by appointment

Stephenson Bell 1992

Stephenson Bell 1992

Career Services Unit (CSU)

Hodder Associates' new CSU building is a welcome addition to a campus not over-blessed with architectural merit. The CSU, established in 1972, previously occupied two sites within the Wilson and Womersley's Precinct Centre, now successfully unified.

Separate from the university, the CSU is a limited company and has two core functions: to provide career advice to graduates, and to design and distribute 'self-selecting' software to university careers advisors. The brief called for accommodation for these two activities and in addition the CSU wanted space for sales and distribution, meeting rooms, executives' suites, and a separate production area.

On a site bound by three uninspiring brick-clad buildings, the architect has designed two rectilinear blocks – unified by a huge *porte-cochère* – arranged at right angles in a traditional collegiate style. This creates a landscaped courtyard, formerly an exposed area of planting, knitting together the dislocated and dreary urban fabric around its perimeter, bringing a new focus point for the campus.

The CSU was designed to respect the scale of both the urban and landscaped areas; the northern elevations address the urban edge, and the southern elevations address the softer and more intimate nature of the courtyard. The north-east elevation is dominated by large-scale elements, such as the open-plan offices that form large cantilevers on *in-situ* barrel vaults. These shadow a wall composed of precast-concrete rainscreen panels, its rhythm broken by a transparent structurally glazed bay window. Internally, the composition of elements creates an interesting office space, with a glazed clerestory at ceiling level that provides high-level cross ventilation and prevents glare from the barrel-vaulted ceiling. Louvred strip windows at seating level give external views.

The south-west elevation is a white rendered façade with louvred strip

Career Services Unit (CSU)

Hodder Associates 1997

windows slicing through its surface. The second storey is set back, creating a recessed 'attic'; that on the south-west elevation provides a roof terrace. Close up, this composition makes the building appear two-storey, thus reducing its scale.

A straight stair from the three-storey entrance foyer provides access to the linear offices; cellular offices face the courtyard and open-plan offices front the hard urban edge. The white render used externally is reflected in the calm and clean detailing inside. The treads of the main stair climb up the wall, held in place by large bolts. The landings and hand-rails are timber, softening the cool steel balustrades.

With a growing national reputation, Stephen Hodder has to be one of the most successful 'new' modernists of his time and place. Exquisitely detailed and formally executed, this building brings life to its tired surroundings and also celebrates the heady days of modernism in a totally contemporary manner.

ADDRESS Prospects House, Booth Street, Manchester [1E 109]
CLIENT Careers Services Unit
STRUCTURAL ENGINEER Blackwood Structural Design
CONTRACT VALUE £1.34 million
SIZE 1162.75 square metres
METROLINK St Peter's Square
BUS 11, 17, 44, 47, 115, 130, 253
ACCESS none

Hodder Associates 1997

Career Services Unit (CSU)

City Centre

Hodder Associates 1997

City Art Gallery

Due for completion in the year 2001, the project – the extension to the gallery and restoration of Charles Barry's nineteenth-century buildings – was enabled by a Lottery application that secured 75 per cent of the funding needed. The design had four elements to it: to provide more space for the collection; to improve public access to the buildings, especially for disabled people (the buildings are 2 metres above street level); to restore Barry's buildings, the main City Art Gallery (1823) and the Athenaeum; and to provide a new building.

Adjoining the Athenaeum, the proposed new building is characterised by two distinct volumes. The end block is the same volume as the Athenaeum and will fill the void between Nicholas Street and George Street, re-establishing the Georgian gridiron street pattern – an important consideration in the conservation area. The central block will be lower, its glass atrium providing the main vertical circulation. The City Art Gallery building will be connected to these volumes via a glass link. Designed for minimum impact with an etched-glass floor and lid, its transparency will reinforce the concept of the street and maximise daylight in the building.

A formal simplicity is again reflected in the internal spaces. For considerable heritage gain the architects wanted to restore as much of Barry's original volumes as possible. The architects also wanted to make the gallery more accessible from the street – windows had previously been blacked out. This has been achieved by housing public facilities on the ground floor, which can benefit from natural light.

The impressive gallery entrance will be retained, with the addition of ramped access. This leads into a retail area with a café to one side. Across the glass link, the new building will house art-education facilities for local school children, and a new loading bay in the central block. A study room

Michael Hopkins and Partners 2001

Michael Hopkins and Partners 2001

for works on paper is proposed for the Athenaeum.

Considering the liabilities involved in the protection of artwork, the most challenging aspect of the brief has been reconciling the lighting and servicing of the buildings. Perhaps the most innovative intervention is the design of a technical roof – top-lit and designed to conserve energy –in the temporary exhibition loft space. The architects and engineers have designed a system that can vary between darkness and total daylight. Light is filtered from high level to provide a general diffuse light (200 lux), with task lighting at lower level to illuminate individual works. Lumen logging will adjust the lighting throughout the day, substituting natural with artificial light as the day draws to a close.

The requirements of a 60-year design life have determined the materials selected for the new building. Its simple concrete frame will be infilled with Derbyshire grit stone set in bronze alloy sub-frames to complement the sandstone of the existing buildings.

Hopkins is no stranger to sensitive contexts as some of his buildings (the Mound Stand at Lords and Glyndebourne Opera House) have eloquently proved. Judging by the precedents borrowed from previous projects such as Shad Thames (concrete frame) and Emanuel College (use of materials), the extension to the gallery will be a contemporary solution that will unify and add freshness to Barry's existing buildings.

ADDRESS Mosley Street, Manchester [a-z]
CLIENT Manchester City Council
STRUCTURAL ENGINEER Ove Arup & Partners
CONTRACT VALUE overall project: £25 million; new building: £16 million
METROLINK St Peter's Square
ACCESS open in 2002

Michael Hopkins and Partners 2001

City Art Gallery

City Centre

Michael Hopkins and Partners 2001

Trinity Court

Trinity Court is neatly situated in a back street, off the main Deansgate route into Manchester. The dramatic Italianate façade, signifying the building's grade-2 listed status, disguises the retail and office spaces discretely housed inside.

The façade is all that remains of the original building, built in 1865 as warehouse and office space. The new building is inserted behind the original façade, gracefully marrying old and new.

The building is 24 metres wide and 37 metres deep, with much-needed car-parking space in the basement and on the ground floor. A stainless-steel-and-glass entrance canopy is an elegant addition to the façade, celebrating the building's past and present functions. A new central atrium, allowing natural daylight to permeate the building, connects the high-quality double-banked offices.

A rich mixture of materials gives the interior space a dignified appeal, with a combination of limestone and sandstone finishes adding quality and durability. The budget was slightly more than average for this type of building, but with the fine selection of materials combined with car-parking space, Trinity Court is no ordinary office development.

ADDRESS 16 John Dalton Street, Manchester [4D 94]
CLIENT John Dalton Partnership
STRUCTURAL ENGINEER YRM Anthony Hunt Associates
CONTRACT VALUE £6.2 million
METROLINK St. Peter's Square
BUS 63, 69, 71, 263, 701
ACCESS none

Stephenson Architecture 1992

Stephenson Architecture 1992

Royal Exchange Theatre

The Royal Exchange Theatre started life in 1809 as a marketplace for more than 6000 cotton traders. It was thought to be one of the largest rooms in the world, boasting a magnificent dome that inspired awe and amazement. Cotton trading long-since ceased, Levitt Bernstein were approached in 1976 to design the original 'space module' theatre space within the great hall, sitting independently of the main exchange building.

The theatre was due to be refurbished in 1996, but after huge damage from the IRA bomb explosion, the company decided to embark on a £30 million renovation programme to upgrade the theatre, including an openable roof allowing acoustics to be manipulated to suit performances.

Entrances to the great hall have been fully redesigned, with the delicate insertion of a glazed enclosure within the original archways and a new lift at the main entrance improving wheelchair access. A 120-seat studio space has been added in the old workshop, which is to be rehoused in a satellite building. The secondary theatre space will provide room for productions to be staged independently of the main theatre. The adjacent restaurant, shops and bars were all extensively redesigned, bringing facilities up to scratch for a theatre of its class.

ADDRESS St Ann's Square, Manchester [4D 94]
CLIENT Royal Exchange Theatre Company
SERVICES ENGINEER Max Fordham & Partners
STRUCTURAL ENGINEER Broadhurst Partnership and Ove Arup & Partners
ACOUSTIC CONSULTANT Arups Acoustics
CONTRACT VALUE £30 million
METROLINK High Street
BUS 7, 8, 32, 34, 63, 64, 94, 114 to Cross Street
ACCESS open

Levitt Bernstein Associates 1998

Levitt Bernstein Associates 1998

Manchester Reform Club

At the heart of Manchester's financial district, and rubbing shoulders with high fashion (Giorgio Armani, DKNY and Joseph) is the Manchester Reform Club. Founded in 1867 by a group of businessmen, the former politician's club was home to the Liberal Party. A symbol of prosperity, it stands as a reminder of the progressive and radical ideas of the time, paying particular tribute to William Gladstone.

Designed by Edward Salomons in 1871, the building is an eclectic rendition of the Venetian Gothic style. The grandeur of its form, with tall arched windows, foliated capitals, and gargoyles, combines both Flemish and Venetian influences, also reflected in its pitched roofs and angular turrets. The former dining room, richly detailed in aged pine panelling, has now been brashly converted into the Reform Bar and Restaurant by Bernard Carroll.

On entering, deep-purple walls and a sweeping oak staircase announce the grotesque make-over to come. The whole scene is salacious and decadent, with materials including red velvet, tiger and leopard prints. Purple and red walls highlight the existing timber and are accompanied by gilded mirrors and custom-designed chandelier-like fittings. Constructed from three chain cylinders and 2.8 metres in length, these break up the 7-metre-high space without obscuring the magnificent panelled ceiling.

The L-shaped main bar/restaurant area is 16-metres wide and 23-metres long with an adjacent clubroom, divided by a curvaceous oak bar that is dominated by a gilded mirror at its centre. A huge 2.3-metre-high red sofa conceals back-of-bar facilities and acts as a sound barrier. A tiger-print 'snake bench' slithers down the centre of the restaurant area; adding to the theme, uplighters are cast-brass female torsos with Pegasus wings, reminiscent of the Jean-Paul Gaultier perfume bottle, a form repeated in the salt pots on the tables. The purity of white tablecloths contrasts

Bernard Carroll 1998

Bernard Carroll 1998

sharply with the red velvet and animal-print furniture.

A reproduction of Renoir's *Boat Party* hangs on the wall. The Reform, definitely not conveying the conviviality depicted in this painting, provides a gaudy alternative to the austere industrial aesthetic first created by Ben Kelly in Dry 201 (see page 6.86). Despite natural light flooding through the tall arched windows during the day, the bar is best experienced at night. Add some black satin sheets and you could almost be in bed with *Changing Rooms'* Laurence Lewellyn Bowen.

ADDRESS King Street, Spring Gardens, Manchester [4D 94]
CONTRACT VALUE £850,000
SIZE 640 square metres
METROLINK St Peter's Square
ACCESS open

Bernard Carroll 1998

Bernard Carroll 1998

Marks & Spencer

The original M&S store was badly damaged in the IRA bomb blast in 1996, necessitating a completely new building. M&S decided to remain in their existing location, and to build their largest store in the world in Manchester. The new store occupies a central position in the newly created city centre and it is incorporated within EDA's winning scheme for the design of the central Manchester masterplan.

A fully glazed footbridge (see page 2.48) designed by Hodder Associates dramatically links Marks and Spencer to the Arndale Centre across Corporation Street, the main shopping centre. Four main entrances located on each side of the building allow direct access into the store and to the underground car park. Planar glazing on the end walls provides stunning views both in and out of the building and on to the redeveloped Exchange Square area. Considerable areas of glazing flood the interior with natural light and large vistas across the building allow shoppers to navigate themselves effortlessly around the store.

ADDRESS Corporation Street, Manchester [3D 94]
CLIENT Marks & Spencer
SIZE 30,000 square metres
CONTRACT VALUE £75 million (estimated)
METROLINK High Street
BUS 18, 21, 28, 68, 88, 93, 94, 167
ACCESS opening hours

Building Design Partnership (BDP) 1999

Marks & Spencer

City Centre

Building Design Partnership (BDP) 1999

Arndale Bridge

Out of the devastation caused by the IRA bomb, which exploded in the centre of Manchester on 15 July 1996, comes the bridge of the future. Its position could not be more significant as it marks the location where the stolen white Ford Cargo van exploded, displacing 670 businesses, injuring 220 people, and destroying the old bridge linking Marks and Spencer with the Arndale Centre.

Taking the form of a hyperbolic paraboloid the new bridge is a progressive vision of the rejuvenated city centre. The bridge is constructed from a lightweight glass membrane with 18 straight steel rods and compression members that appear to twist around its surface, in both clockwise and anti-clockwise directions. Its symmetrical geometry redresses the change in the level of the broadwalk running through its centre between the two shopping areas. Stretching across Corporation Street, the bridge's arched form also maximises visibility and allows uninterrupted views of the street and beyond.

This bridge from one of Manchester's highly acclaimed architectural practices is a radical and forward-looking solution that demonstrates the city's ability to transform itself.

ADDRESS Corporation Street, Manchester [3D 94]
CLIENT Manchester City Council
STRUCTURAL ENGINEER Ove Arup & Partners
CONTRACT VALUE £600,000
SIZE 20 metres long
METROLINK High Street
ACCESS open

Hodder Associates 1999

Arndale Bridge

City Centre

Hodder Associates 1999

Tampopo

The Tampopo noodle bar is a welcome addition to Manchester's diverse and flourishing restaurant scene. Situated in the main public square, adjacent to Alfred Waterhouse's splendid Gothic town hall, Tampopo can be found in a converted basement beneath the street. Discreet and taciturn signage announces the restaurant's presence at street level, and narrow windows offer select glimpses of activity above the dining area.

The restaurant is concealed behind a sleek door at the base of a natural timber staircase. Once inside, the large open-plan restaurant contrasts strongly with its status as a basement venue, a spacious and unpretentious place to eat. Functional, slender wooden tables create a no-frills, non-hierarchical atmosphere. The kitchen workspace is at the rear of the restaurant; a chest-high counter separates the two activities but carefully avoids obscuring the theatre of preparation and cooking.

Clever deployment of artificial and natural lighting introduces warmth to the interior, complementing the cleanliness of the wall planes. Hard and soft materials combined with the restrained use of colour offset the coolness so often associated with minimalist interiors.

The success of the restaurant and its interior is a tribute to the architects' skill in their first foray into an interior of this nature. Tampopo will be a hard act to follow, an ideal setting for the synthesis of eastern and western cuisine, proving that minimalist interiors need not be austere.

ADDRESS Albert Square, Manchester [4D 94]
CLIENT Tampopo Ltd
CONTRACT VALUE £100,000
BUS 7, 8, 32, 34, 63, 64, 94, 114 to Cross Street
ACCESS check opening hours

Harrison Ince 1997

Harrison Ince 1997

201 Deansgate

Deansgate is one of the city's main arterial routes, carrying a heavy volume of traffic throughout the day. This office development is half way down Deansgate as you enter Manchester from the south.

The mixed-use ground floor of the building promotes diverse activity at street level, in keeping with planning policy, and five upper floors total 6350 square metres of high-quality office space. Car parking for more than 90 vehicles is at basement and ground levels. An additional 700 square metres is taken up by archive space for tenants in the lower basement.

The building has a robust character; it takes its vertical form from the surrounding urban landscape, signalling a strong architectural presence to its neighbours. A delightful atrium, creating a light and airy atmosphere, overwhelms the visitor on entry. Spectacular views deep into the building further emphasise its verticality, and create a link to street activity. The use and combination of materials – red sandstone, steel, glass and red brick – are its most remarkable feature, giving a contemporary feel to the building, while respecting the city's architectural legacy.

The finished building, already a noted part of the Deansgate skyline, is a tribute to the collective energy of the participants.

ADDRESS 201 Deansgate, Manchester [4D 94]
CLIENT Chestergate Seddon Ltd
STRUCTURAL ENGINEER Modus
CONTRACT VALUE £7.8 million
METROLINK St Peter's Square
BUS 5, 35, 46, 63, 71, 114, 131
ACCESS limited

Holford Associates 1996

City Centre

Holford Associates 1996

Trinity Bridge

This is one of the most stunning bridges to be found anywhere in the UK, linking the semi-derelict hinterland of Salford – an area currently undergoing major regeneration – with Manchester City Centre. The Civic Trust voted Calatrava's bridge the best public/private sector partnership project in the country, giving a boost to this forgotten area of the city.

Access to the bridge from the Manchester side of the River Irwell is via Parsonage Gardens, in the backwater behind Lewis' department store, just off Deansgate. The bridge, with its 41-metre-high rotund pylon, creates an immediate impact on the Salford skyline. Anchored to the Salford side of the footbridge, the inclined pylon supports the hollow box-girder deck below by steel stay cables. The bridge has a graceful appearance when illuminated after dark by its circular lamps, positioned where the cables connect to the anchors in the centre of the main deck.

The immediate area around the bridge was carefully landscaped with block-floor paving and bespoke street furniture, allowing pedestrians to sit and chat or view the bridge's different aspects from various viewing points. When fully developed, Chapel Wharf will be a vibrant area bustling with activity, with Calatrava's footbridge creating an elegant link between the two cities.

ADDRESS Chapel Wharf, Salford [3D 94]
CLIENT Salford City Council
ENGINEER Salford City Council
METROLINK St Peter's Square, then a 5-minute walk
BR Salford
ACCESS open

Santiago Calatrava 1994

Santiago Calatrava 1994

Peoples' History Museum

Forget six countries overhung with smoke.
Forget the smoking steam and piston stroke.
William Morris, 1868, quoted in the museum

This museum is dedicated to 'Britain's first Industrial Working Class'; from the battle for factory reform in Lancashire's cotton mills in the eighteenth century to the ambulance-workers' dispute of 1989, it documents working people's lives and narrates their fight for democracy. Relocated from Limehouse Town Hall in east London, this conversion, next to the River Irwell in Manchester's only remaining Edwardian pumphouse, provides a permanent site for the collection whose exhibits include the largest assortment of trade union banners, Labour Party papers and domestic artefacts.

The architect's approach to the brief has demonstrated the same amount of confidence as the construction of the existing building – which supplied hydraulic power to much of Manchester's industry until its closure in 1972 – shows. This confidence has been achieved by working respectfully with the masonry and steel fabric of the building while giving solid expression to the new insertions.

The former engine room marks the entry sequence to the museum's permanent and temporary galleries, and accommodates the main reception, bookshop and café, unified by a floating lid. The main focal point is the liftshaft at the back of the room providing disabled access to the temporary galleries. Situated along the central axis, balconies slot into its red-brick surface providing viewing platforms over the main entrance. OMI's use of *blanc de bierge* concrete and red-brick planar elements which slide into each other along steel I-beams makes the circulation route even clearer. Emphasising a building in motion, these shifting planes signpost

OMI 1993

OMI 1993

the permanent gallery entrance, positioned next to the lift shaft.

The deep plan of the 6-metre-high permanent gallery has been divided by a mezzanine level, suspended via diagonal ties from beams that once supported the watertanks of the boilerhouse. In order to preserve the sensitive exhibits, this space is totally windowless. Blocked off by a wall, the original windows now form a glazed façade to the River Irwell, giving room for a narrow stair corridor rising to the temporary exhibition galleries. Entering this space from the permanent exhibition is like coming out of a cinema on a sunny day.

The temporary galleries occupy the original coal store. Split in two, the upper level is characterised by an A-frame roof, and has voids around its floor perimeter with unrestricted views of the gallery space below. Vertical circulation is provided by a spiral stair enclosed in a chunky white cylinder that obstructs the vista to the riverfront, adding to the sense of discovery. The view is then restored by a triangular window projecting out of the façade, with an exclusive view of Calatrava's footbridge (see page 2.54) further down the River Irwell.

ADDRESS The Pumphouse, Left Bank, Bridge Street, Manchester [4C 94]
CLIENT The National Museum of Labour History Exhibition
STRUCTURAL ENGINEER Buro Happold
CONTRACT VALUE £1 million
METROLINK St Peter's Square
BR Salford Central
ACCESS open

OMI 1993

OMI 1993

Granada Studios

Granada TV is the north-west's main regional broadcasting centre, home to many of the nation's favourite programmes, including *Coronation Street*, a 30-year-old soap opera set in a fictional town modelled on a close-knit community in Salford. With the increasing popularity of its programmes, Granada opened up the studios so that visitors can see the set's inner workings, with the added bonus of enjoying a drink in the Rovers' Return.

Needing to expand its site, Granada converted an adjoining warehouse on Grape Street, originally constructed for the London and North Western Railway Company in 1867–69. The massive Victorian warehouse provided the ideal backdrop for period dramas and productions. Granada also required a 4000-square-metre production studio, complete with back-up facilities for 200 actors, administration areas and adequate storage space for filming equipment. The exterior fabric of the building has been fully restored, which is important due to it being highly visible from the end of the relocated and rebuilt Coronation Street set.

Numerous layers of whitewash were removed from the interior walls, revealing the original brickwork, and the floor was blasted clean, again to display the brick and timber of the building's heritage.

ADDRESS Grape Street, Manchester [5C 94]
CLIENT Granada Television
STRUCTURAL ENGINEER Building Design Partnership
SIZE 13,500 square metres
METROLINK G-MEX
ACCESS Granada Television Studios Tour

Building Design Partnership (BDP) 1984

Building Design Partnership (BDP) 1984

G-MEX Centre

The Greater Manchester Exhibition and Event Centre (G-MEX) came into existence in July 1880 as Central Station Main Train Hall. When complete, it became Manchester's fourth railway terminal, a bustling and vibrant interchange of traffic, goods and passengers on the Ancoats branch of the Midland line.

In 1963 Central Station was grade-2 listed; later in the '60s the station fell victim to cuts in the national railway system, closing in 1969. In the late 1970s Manchester City Council commissioned EGS to undertake an extensive feasibility study for redevelopment of the area and Central Station, including Bridgewater Hall opposite (see page 2.64). After six years of negotiation, G-MEX finally opened in 1986. G-MEX features 18 main wrought-iron arch frames, spanning 65 metres in length, and more than 25 metres high. These provide a massive area of flexible floor space, allowing conferences, exhibitions and performances to be staged.

With 750 car-parking spaces beneath the centre, external courtyards can be left free if an exhibition requires more floorspace above. With the majority of parking below, the restored G-MEX can be fully appreciated by road-traffic and Metrolink passengers entering the city centre.

ADDRESS Lower Mosley Street, Manchester [5D 94]
CLIENT Greater Manchester Council
ENGINEERS Brian Colquhoun & Partners
METROLINK St Peter's Square
BR Oxford Road
ACCESS contact G-MEX for details

EGS Design 1986

EGS Design 1986

Bridgewater Hall

Manchester is internationally renowned for its contribution to the dance-music and street-fashion scenes. In an attempt to raise the city's profile as a choral and orchestral music venue, Manchester City Council decided to establish a new concert hall. With £42 million allocated from governmental and European sources, RHWL won the Bridgewater Initiative competition in 1990 to create a suitable building for the clients' aspirations to international status, to stand alongside the striking architecture of G-MEX .

The Bridgewater is a free-standing structure, on a red sandstone plinth, with the Rochdale Canal to its rear and the main Metrolink line opposite. Pointing north towards Albert Square in the city, public access is through a glazed entrance, suspended beneath a stainless-steel prow. Organised on two tiers, the foyers are linked by a main staircase, with views into the auditorium space. The 2400-seat central auditorium space takes references from Scharoun's Berlin Philarmonie and von Hansen's Musikvereinsgebäude in Vienna. The architect worked closely with Arup Acoustics to design a space that enhanced the quality of sound during performances and created visual interconnectedness between audience and musicians.

ADDRESS Lower Mosley Street, Manchester [5D 94]
CLIENT Manchester City Council
STRUCTURAL ENGINEERS Ove Arup & Partners
SEATING CONSULTANTS Audience Systems
LIGHTING DESIGN Lighting Design Partnership
CONTRACT VALUE £42 million
BUS 101, 104, 106, 109
METROLINK G-MEX
ACCESS CHECK WITH BOX OFFICE

RHWL Partnership 1996

City Centre

RHWL Partnership 1996

Green Room Theatre, Phase 2

For more than ten years the Green Room Theatre has occupied two arches beneath a busy railway line near the Cornerhouse Arts Centre. Acclaimed for its experimental productions, this fringe theatre is an integral part of Manchester's cultural scene. A significant amount of Lottery funding in 1995 enabled the client to refurbish the theatre space and café-bar.

On arrival at the theatre, you can choose between two entrances, to the box office to the left or the café-bar to the right. Both façades use stainless-steel panels and slate-grey windows that contrast boldly with the surrounding brickwork. The lightweight steel mezzanine level adds much-needed floorspace to the café-bar. To satisfy fire regulations, the architect used this level as a means of escape to a new fire exit on to Great Marlborough Street.

The vinyl sheet flooring, stainless-steel bar and the oak staircase, combined with the sensitive use of lighting, create an airy but intimate space. The imaginative use of signage and interactive artwork add richness and a sense of play to the interior. The compact auditorium, seating more than 120, is tucked behind the foyer area; greatly improved acoustics and a new seating arrangement together provide a remarkable theatre space.

ADDRESS Whitworth Street West, Manchester [5D 94]
CLIENT The Green Room Theatre
STRUCTURAL ENGINEER Eric Bassett Associates
CONTRACT VALUE £643,000
METROLINK G-MEX
BUS 101, 104, 106, 109, 124, 250
ACCESS check opening times prior to visiting

Ian Simpson Architects 1996

Ian Simpson Architects 1996

Manchester Metrolink

It is hard to imagine a single element making a more dramatic impact on the cityscape and working life of Manchester than the Metrolink Light Railway Transportation System. Within a relatively short period, the Metrolink trams have become a popular means of transport, attracting more than 13 million passengers a year. Statistics collected by the GMPTE show that peak-time road traffic has fallen by 6 per cent.

The 26-kilometre Metrolink begins in Altrincham, the affluent suburb south of the city, and runs along Railtrack lines until the G-MEX stop. Then it switches to purpose-built tracks laid in the road, taking the trams into the heart of the city, to Piccadilly mainline station or north to Bury. Stops are frequent and passengers' needs are catered for with carriage flooring at the same height as the platforms and designated areas for wheelchair users and those with prams.

Murano shelters, designed by a subsidiary of J C Decaux, the French company, have been used, providing adequate shelter for passengers waiting on the platforms. Fares are competitive – tickets must be bought before travelling.

Phase 2 – from Manchester through to Eccles in Salford – opens up a vital corridor, linking the city to Salford Quays and beyond, and providing easy access to Dumplington shopping centre and The Lowry (see page 7.6). If successful, many more routes are planned for the Metrolink, providing an extensive tram network for Manchester, and an integrated public transportation system unrivalled anywhere in the UK.

CONTRACT VALUE £130 million
ROUTE Altrincham to Bury
ACCESS fare-paying passengers only

GMPTE 1992

Fallowfield to Altrincham

Callooh! Callay!

Callooh! Callay! café-bar is in a quiet street in the centre of Altrincham, a small and affluent town on the periphery of south Manchester. The café-bar is ideally positioned to provide a break for beleaguered shoppers with children and visitors to the area. Its name derives from the poem 'The Jabberwock' in Lewis Carroll's *Through the Looking Glass*, giving a clue to what's in store.

The delightful interior-design scheme was the result of a clearly defined brief, consolidated by thorough research in the initial stages, and close collaboration with Stephen Graham, the interior designer. It had to be durable to survive the constant knocks of children's activity, changeable to feature artworks of varying sizes, and informal but lively to accommodate kids and their parents.

Arranged on ground and basement levels, every square metre of floor space has been carefully utilised. Access can be gained via the main entrance on the central axis or the ramped access to the side, catering for wheelchair users and parents with buggies. The ground floor is divided into two distinct areas of activity: eating and playing. Tables and seating are carefully arranged on either side of the entrance towards the front of the café-bar, a relaxed, informal space to eat and drink, and a visual link to the outside street. To the rear is Art-works, a distinct area of activity devoted to children's play and crèche facilities, positioned at the furthest point away from the main entrance, with an eye to security and supervision.

The basement houses toilets, office space and an area devoted to hosting private children's parties. Lively and fresh, it continues with the theme used throughout the ground floor, and does not suffer from the inherent problems of basement rooms: poor lighting and a sense of claustrophobia.

Stephen Graham, Alison and Andrew Brownlee 1996

Fallowfield to Altrincham

Stephen Graham, Alison and Andrew Brownlee 1996

Callooh! Callay!

Materials used throughout the café-bar include white painted plaster walls, soft timber flooring and smooth wipe-clean surfaces. Quotations from *Through the Looking Glass* are featured on the walls, adding a subtle sense of discovery for the visitor while also bringing an element of eccentricity to the interior.

Callooh! Callay! offers an innovative solution to an enduring problem – there is no finer example of a café-bar for parents and children to eat and play, all contained within an uncompromisingly cool and modern environment. And there is more: it provides a one-stop, supervised activity centre for children, and the opportunity to peruse and purchase contemporary artworks.

ADDRESS 28–32 Greenwood Street, Altrincham [1F 145]
CLIENTS Alison and Andrew Brownlee
SIZE 353 square metres
BUS 11, 17, 245, 263, 264, 268
ACCESS Sunday to Thursday, 10.00–18.00; Friday, Saturday, until late

Stephen Graham, Alison and Andrew Brownlee 1996

Stephen Graham, Alison and Andrew Brownlee 1996

Hollins Library, Manchester Metropolitan University

The 'toaster', 'rasher of bacon' and 'fried egg' are a collection of buildings synonymous with Manchester Metropolitan University. Nicknamed because of their quite literal form, the 'fried egg' (formerly an under-utilised examination hall) has been replaced by the new Hollins Library which is located in the same position. Following the Follet Report, the project was grant-assisted by the Higher Education Council, and is a response to the growing trend in Learning Resource Centres (LRCS). The appointment of the architect followed the successful and highly acclaimed development of the curvaceous Aytoun Street Library (see page 2.16) for the same institution in the city centre.

The new library continues the culinary theme: it now resembles an electric chip fryer, especially from above. Two storeys higher than the previous 'egg', its circular façade is softened by terracotta render, a departure from the white Meier-esque purity of the architect's previous Siemens and Aytoun Library projects. Sitting comfortably with its neighbours, the LRC is a nucleus of modern learning, relegating the 1960s relics around its circumference to the archives.

Internally, the space is calm and tranquil, the intense concentration of its core activity lifted by the constant stream of daylight flooding into its sealed envelope. Spatial configuration is clear and concise, made simpler by the bicycle-wheel form of the skeletal steel frame supporting the roof. This has removed the need for a central column, thus freeing up space. All bookshelves and desks are designed to harmonise with the spatial geometry. The lower ground floor forms an enclosed computer room with terminals placed all around its perimeter. Access to the library is via the middle floor, reducing staffing levels.

At Hollins, like other MBLC projects, there is a strong resonance with

Mills Beaumont Leavey Channon (MBLC) 1995

Mills Beaumont Leavey Channon (MBLC) 1995

3.8

the work of Richard Meier. The third floor is an impressive double-height space with a void with views over the reading room below.

Despite being criticised for not pushing the environmental agenda, and so resulting in increased running and maintenance costs for the university, the building has received a very positive reaction from both clients and users. Indeed, like the Aytoun Library, this building not only significantly improves the university's facilities and image but also provides a modern, progressive and uplifting place in which to study.

Fallowfield to Altrincham

ADDRESS Old Hall Lane (off Wilmslow Road), Manchester M14 [6H 109]
CLIENT Manchester Metropolitan University
STRUCTURAL ENGINEER Modus Consulting Engineers
CONTRACT VALUE £2.1 million
SIZE 1875 square metres
BUS 40–44, 48, 140, 142, 155, 157
ACCESS limited

Mills Beaumont Leavey Channon (MBLC) 1995

Hollins Library, Manchester Metropolitan University

Fallowfield to Altrincham

Mills Beaumont Leavey Channon (MBLC) 1995

J Sainsbury and John Lewis Partnership

This out-of-town shopping development is situated on the recently completed A34 bypass and was built primarily to serve the affluent middle-class population of the 'stockbroker belt' of south Manchester and north Cheshire – the leafy suburbs of Bowdon, Hale Barns, Bramhall and Wilmslow. With the Trafford Centre open, attracting thousands of people from the surrounding catchment areas, this mini-mall offers an alternative for local shoppers and an ideal pitstop for those travelling to Manchester Airport only two miles away.

The joint retail development covers a 29-acre site, and comprises a three-storey department store for the John Lewis Partnership and a single-storey Sainsbury's supermarket, unified by a double-height glazed link, the focal point of the development which provides access to each store. This link overlooks an extensively landscaped car park, where native and ornamental trees and shrubs were added to existing planting.

The close proximity of the airport has clearly influenced the design – overhead flight paths determined the building's orientation on the site. Diners in the first-floor restaurant/coffee bar in the glazed link can observe both ground and air traffic. The aerodynamic form of the steel eyebrow detail to the glazed clerestorey resembles the wing of an aircraft – a theme used consistently throughout. However, this aviation theme is comprised by a form recalling an air-traffic control tower, marking the junction with a trolley store that awkwardly interrupts the lines of the building.

Each store's identity is clearly expressed, not only in scale and corporate identity but also in materiality and detailing. Set back from the John Lewis store via the glazed link, the Sainsbury's façade is fully glazed, one of their trademarks. This is in contrast with the John Lewis elevation, a sandstone wall under the glass and steel clerestory.

Percy Thomas Partnership (Architects) Limited 1997

J Sainsbury and John Lewis Partnership

Fallowfield to Altrincham

Percy Thomas Partnership (Architects) Limited 1997

J Sainsbury and John Lewis Partnership

Reconciling the differences in scale between the two buildings has not been fully resolved, though an attempt has been made with a chunky white canopy that marries the glazed link with the supermarket. Nonetheless, the retail development is a welcome contribution to the area.

ADDRESS between A34 Kingsway and B5358 at junction with Etchells Road, Cheadle, Cheshire [3H 149]
CLIENTS J Sainsbury and the John Lewis Partnership
CONTRACT VALUE £18 million
BUS 127, 130, 155, 157, 170, 312
ACCESS open

Percy Thomas Partnership (Architects) Limited 1997

J Sainsbury and John Lewis Partnership

Fallowfield to Altrincham

Percy Thomas Partnership (Architects) Limited 1997

Sir Geoffrey Manton Building, Manchester Metropolitan University

Manchester Metropolitan University already has a reputation for commissioning innovative architecture (see page 2.16) and the Geoffrey Manton Building is a strong addition to their portfolio.

Sheppard Robson designed the masterplan for the All Saints campus (Site 3) in 1976 and the development of this teaching facility for the Humanities Department, situated on the campus' south-east corner, gave them an opportunity to readdress the site. The brief called for adaptable space for students and staff to suit the university's changing needs; to reurbanise the campus within its city site; and to integrate all buildings on the campus.

Like many university campuses, Site 3 had grown organically, resulting in the fragmentation that was one of the architects' key concerns. Using the new building as a catalyst for change, the architects restored a sense of faculty community by designing a largely inward-facing building, a common approach in educational design. With a collegiate-courtyard form, the building is arranged around a huge atrium, with a clear dialogue between functions and spaces.

Turning its back on Oxford Road, the main entrance directly engages with the rest of the campus buildings. Leading into the atrium space, this entrance has been given a focus by the dynamic juxtaposition of a triangular section, also highlighting the bridged link to the Mabel Tylecote Building, part of the same faculty. This triangular form is reflected on the other side of the building: diametrically opposite in plan, it punctuates the southern tip of the campus to Oxford Road. This diagonal is emphasised internally by the central position of a semi-circular dogleg stair, and the curved lattice roof structure. These elements, together with its volume, make the atrium a dramatic space.

Sheppard Robson 1996

Sir Geoffrey Manton Building, Manchester Metropolitan University

Fallowfield to Altrincham

Sheppard Robson 1996

Sir Geoffrey Manton Building, Manchester Metropolitan University

In addition to providing the main circulation route, the atrium is a display and exhibition space, its success highlighted by the number of television companies that have hired it for shoots. Embracing the university's 'open-door policy' and preventing the building from being completely introspective, the atrium is visible from Oxford Road, promoting a relationship with the city, and the use of red brick reflects the building's context.

Constructed using a modular discipline, the building is planned to be flexible, avoiding the traditional plan form in favour of non-cellular construction techniques. Large-span structural elements are employed to maximise open-plan space, the only hard areas are circulation and service cores. To optimise on energy efficiency natural light and ventilation are used where possible, the only exceptions being the ground-floor lecture theatre and the computer suite. Academic and departmental accommodation has been divided – staff rooms on the upper floors have panoramic views over the city, while students occupy the lower floors.

A bold gesture, this building respects the Mancunian tradition and also meets the university's changing requirements for the new century.

ADDRESS Rosamond Street West, off Oxford Road, Manchester M15 [1E 109]
CLIENT Manchester Metropolitan University,
STRUCTURAL ENGINEER Ove Arup & Partners
CONTRACT VALUE £11.5 million
SIZE 13,000 square metres
BUS 11, 16, 40, 42, 114, 254, 263
ACCESS limited

Sheppard Robson 1996

Fallowfield to Altrincham

Sheppard Robson 1996

Sir William Siemens House

Siemens is an internationally recognised blue-chip company at the forefront of technological development. In the late 1980s the company identified a need for a new site for their Energy and Automation division, opting for the strategically important Princess Road location. Siemens was insistent that the new site should provide easy access to the main motorway network and that it should be suitable for further development in the future.

Situated opposite the massive Manchester Southern Cemetery, adjoined by low-level housing, Siemens was designed and landscaped to cause minimum visual disruption to the surrounding landscape. While remaining sensitive to its neighbours, it also acts as a gateway to Manchester, providing a landmark to road traffic entering and leaving the centre.

The building grid is based on two strong geometries. The first of these is dictated by the tree-lined avenues found opposite in the cemetery across Princess Road. The second takes its cue from the nearby Withington Hospital, providing a sensitive dialogue with the existing urban fabric. Floor area of the first phase is an impressive 13,400 square metres, with parking space available for more than 400 cars. Rather than use a tarmac surface for parking, the architects have used natural millstone, so reducing costly site work when the first phase is extended.

The elegance of the Siemens building stems from its simplicity and dignity, primarily achieved through its dynamic form. Three intersecting geometric forms are grouped around a central courtyard. Housed within these are offices, a restaurant, conference facilities and an exhibition area.

A circular four-storey element contains the main entrance and reception, training school and management. This is connected to more office

Mills Beaumont Leavey Channon 1990

Fallowfield to Altrincham

Mills Beaumont Leavey Channon 1990

Sir William Siemens House

space and the restaurant across the courtyard via a delicate four-storey glass walkway, linking the three elements into one cohesive structure.

The building is clad in aluminium rainscreen, giving it an overall appearance of lightness, transparency and delicacy, that will wear evenly through weathering, exhibiting the patina of time.

ADDRESS Princes Road [4C 124]
CLIENT Siemens plc (Energy and Automation Division)
STRUCTURAL ENGINEER Modus
CONTRACT VALUE £8 million
SIZE 13,400 square metres (phase 1)
BUS 46, 47, 84, 129, 169, 171, 172
ACCESS none

Mills Beaumont Leavey Channon 1990

Sir William Siemens House

Mills Beaumont Leavey Channon 1990

Fallowfield to Altrincham

Hulme to Stretford

201 City Road Surgery

201 City Road is in the St George's area of Hulme, a district of bleak inner-city housing designated for regeneration. As part of Hulme's City Challenge Initiative the architects have designed a building that contributes to this process and fulfils the city's desire to provide a better and safer environment for local people.

Hulme's chequered history and reputation for drug-related crime and poor living conditions meant that the most challenging part of the architect's brief was how to provide a secure environment for staff and patients without succumbing to a siege mentality. The client was unhappy with her previous premises and wanted a solution which would provide accommodation large enough for two GPs, a trainee and a practice nurse, with the addition of meeting rooms and office space.

The building is situated between 1950s local-authority housing, a four-storey terrace to the north-west of the site and a row of terraces to the north-east. By responding thoughtfully to the scale of the surrounding area the architect has designed a two-storey building that is not only impregnable to drug thieves, but that also provides a welcoming and comfortable environment.

To meet the City Challenge Initiative requirements the surgery had to work at street level and reinforce the building line; this has been successfully achieved. Externally, a series of architectural mechanisms cleverly manipulate the building's scale, giving it greater impact on the street. The most impressive statement is a boomerang roof; with its 'v' balanced upon a column above the exposed steel lintel of the recessed entrance, it appears to hover above the building. This impression of detachment is enhanced by a glazed clerestory that allows light to filter through the building. Of 'plywood stressed-skin monocoque construction', the roof is an excellent deterrent to burglars. Its form and materiality soften the formality of the

Hodder Associates 1996

Hodder Associates 1996

red-brick façade which is interrupted by glass-block glazing allowing more light into the building. Steel louvres behind the first floor glazing and the use of *brise-soleils* minimise solar gain while acting as security grilles.

On the ground floor the cellular rooms have been arranged sequentially on either side of an internal corridor progressing from public to private space. This transition marks the patient's road to recovery – from reception to diagnosis and finally treatment. The waiting room is a double-height space, light, spacious and informal, encouraging relaxation. This contrasts with the more intimate consultation and treatment rooms, with glass block and structurally glazed laylighting providing a more diffuse level of light to increase the sense of confidentiality. Patients can leave the building at the back which is opposite a park, or via a side entrance to the car park.

This building, executed with a strong emphasis on egalitarian values, embraces the modernist ideals of Berthold Lubetkin. It provides a humanitarian environment designed to meet the needs of modern healthcare, giving hope to an area fraught with social problems.

ADDRESS 201 City Road, Hulme, Manchester [1A 108]
CLIENT Dr Mary Gibbs
STRUCTURAL ENGINEER Clark Smith Partnership
CONTRACT VALUE £235,000
BUS 256, 257, 259, 263
ACCESS none

Hodder Associates 1996

Hodder Associates 1996

Zion Arts Centre

Bright and playful, the Zion Arts Centre occupies an Edwardian former church at the heart of the Hulme Regeneration Area. Built in 1911, the building has been redeveloped to provide dance and music facilities for young people, including studio space for rudimentary ballet classes for 4–5 year olds and rehearsal rooms for national orchestras and choirs.

The church has always been a place of assembly and has had many uses: the number of deaths during the Blitz in World War 2 decreased its congregation substantially in the 1940s and it then became the main rehearsal space for Manchester's Hallé Orchestra. With the orchestra relocating to a purpose-built home in the Bridgewater Hall (see page 2.64), a new use had to be found for the building.

Part of the council's Hulme redevelopment initiative, Zion Arts Centre's phased regeneration was made possible through Lottery and ERDF funding. Phase I was primarily concerned with the creation of a new public entrance to the centre and the modernisation of the existing performance spaces. The architects have achieved this by exploiting the building's generous volumes and acoustic qualities and unifying its chaotic layout.

The new entrance is cheerful and welcoming and has been formed by remodelling the ground and basement spaces at the front of the building. The partial removal of the ground floor has created a 7.5-metre-high space, allowing light from the double-height vaulted windows to flood into the previously hidden basement area. This space is bridged by a curved ramp constructed from two truss frames that form its deck structure and balustrades. The outer balustrade is clad in perforated metal, the inner balustrade in toughened glass panels, and the deck in machine-grooved, kiln-dried southern white pine.

As well as improving access, the ramp also entices people into the

Mills Beaumont Leavey Channon 1997 (phase 1)

Hulme to Stretford

Mills Beaumont Leavey Channon 1997 (phase 1)

building from the main entrance and adds to the playful nature of the space, further emphasised by a 64-square-metre yellow, red, and blue resin canvas on the basement floor, 2 metres below street level. The warren of performance spaces in the basement can be reached either by the existing stair or the new lift in the extended foyer. Of particular interest on this level are two music-rehearsal rooms whose curved glass-block walls enliven the adjacent corridor space.

The detailing has been kept simple, with bold primary colours complimented by clean contemporary elements. In some areas, however, the overall concept has been compromised by poor workmanship and lack of attention to detail.

Phase 2, also complete, involves the renovation of the main auditorium to provide more creative facilities for the young people of Hulme and Greater Manchester.

ADDRESS Stretford Road, Hulme, Manchester M16 [1C 108]
CLIENT Moss Side and Hulme Partnership
STRUCTURAL ENGINEERS Phase 1 – David Crossley Associates; Phase 2 – Steven Hunt and Associates
CONTRACT VALUE Phase 1 – £ 1 million; Phase 2 – £ 894,000
BUS 17, 53, 114, 115, 253, 254
ACCESS open

Mills Beaumont Leavey Channon 1997 (phase 1)

Mills Beaumont Leavey Channon 1997 (phase 1)

Homes for Change

Homes for Change are situated where the infamous crescent deck-access maisonettes once stood. This new model of co-operative social housing has taken their place, providing accommodation for large and small families, single parents and first-time buyers. Fully involved throughout all stages of its development, the co-op members demanded a housing scheme that fulfilled their varied needs, with a strong emphasis on social integration and communal activity '18 hours a day'.

The first phase features 50 flats of varied sizes to suit diverse lifestyles, providing the development with a richness and vibrancy that is so often missing from social housing schemes in the UK. Built in a U-shaped layout, the flats surround a central courtyard designed for social activity and special events and maintained by the residents. Despite the failings of its predecessor, the developers have managed to satisfy residents' wishes to have deck-access housing, carefully linking all the four- and six-storey buildings together.

Materials for the flats were chosen for minimal maintenance, hard wear, affordability and, most importantly, environmental friendliness. The sensitive use of hard and soft materials provides the development with an unusualness and sophistication that belie its tight budget.

ADDRESS Royce Road, Hulme, Manchester [1C 108]
DEVELOPER Guinness Trust Housing Association
STRUCTURAL ENGINEERS YRM Anthony Hunt Associates
BUS 253, 254, 256, 257, 259
ACCESS

Mills Beaumont Leavey Channon 1996

Mills Beaumont Leavey Channon 1996

Boundary Lane

Since the demolition of the notorious 1960s system-built housing estate, Hulme has undergone radical changes through its physical development and has emerged as a vibrant gateway to the centre of the city. Here, after a lengthy consultation process with tenants and the local authority, the architects have created a robust housing scheme, diverse in character.

The development consists of a wide variety of living units, complete with a complex arrangement of public and private spaces, dominated by the housing office, an important central reference point for tenants. The construction of the housing blocks engenders surprise yet remains familiar, a response to the previous monotonous urban environment which reflects tenants' wishes. A sense of security and safety is promoted by positioning living rooms overlooking the public realm.

Porches, walls and bin stores are carefully blended into the fabric of the scheme, demonstrating attention to detail and the interrelationship of architecture and landscape was clearly foremost in the designer's mind. Materials were selected for durability and cost-effectiveness; red brick-work reflects the Manchester vernacular.

OMI should be congratulated on their approach to revitalising the scarred landscape of Hulme. The Boundary Lane development placed the values and needs of the tenants first through all its stages.

ADDRESS Boundary Lane, Hulme, Manchester [1E 109]
CLIENT The Guinness Trust
STRUCTURAL ENGINEER Curtins Consulting Engineers plc
CONTRACT VALUE £7.5 million
BUS 114, 115, 260, 263, 290, 291
ACCESS none

OMI Architects 1997

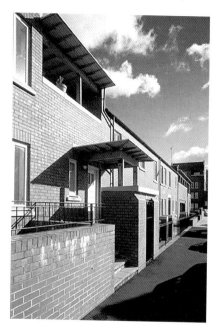

OMI Architects 1997

Hulme Arch Bridge

Chris Wilkinson's bridge is a key structure in the regeneration of Hulme. The bridge, a mile south of the city, spans Princess Road, the major arterial route from the city centre to the main motorway network. It is ideally placed to indicate the changing significance of the area to all road traffic travelling beneath the bridge, both in and out of the city.

The single steel arch rises an impressive 25 metres above deck level and 32 metres from Princess Road beneath it. Diagonally rotated, with a 50-metre span, it allows traffic to travel in both directions along Stretford Road, while maintaining a strong sense of presence. Slender spiral-strand steel cables support the main deck below.

The Hulme Arch Bridge successfully demonstrates that dramatic architectural gestures can maintain their elegance through 'clarity of intent' and simplicity. The bridge is a fitting complement to Hulme's regeneration plans, a focal point to the gateway of the city.

ADDRESS Stretford Road, Hulme, Manchester [1D 108]
CLIENT Hulme Regeneration Company
ENGINEER Ove Arup & Partners
BUS 17, 53, 114, 115, 253, 254
ACCESS open

Chris Wilkinson Architects 1990

Hulme Arch Bridge

Chris Wilkinson Architects 1990

Rolls Crescent

Rolls Crescent stands on the former Crescent Blocks, a system-built, deck-access development that lead to segregation, anonymity and alienation. The new scheme, developed in consultation with the Crescent Blocks' previous residents, follows the principles set down by the Hulme Redevelopment Guide. This has resulted in 67 dwellings designed to promote a sense of community, identity and membership with the rest of the city.

With a clear distinction between public and private space, a selection of one-, two- and three-bedroom dwellings is arranged around three enclosed central courtyards (one on each block). Each dwelling faces outwards with either a private garden or a roof terrace to the rear that backs on to a central meeting place, encouraging neighbourhood surveillance – the scheme complies with the Building Research Establishment's 'Secure by Design' standards.

Following traditional street patterns, the three-storey dwellings are placed along primary roads and the two-storey dwellings along secondary roads. The corner of the perimeter blocks is marked by a three-storey tower, giving focus and visual legibility to each block. These towers have been made more distinctive by using different colour render (rust in contrast to cream) and a boomerang roof detail, contrasting with the curved silver aluminium roof decks of the neighbouring dwellings. Bay and corner windows with exposed steel frames were used to increase surveillance by offering views up and down the street. Two- and four-person bungalows with adjacent steel and glass carports have been provided for disabled people.

An important aspect of the city's development strategy is sustainability, so all the materials used were selected for low maintenance and durability, and all the dwellings were designed with energy efficiency in mind.

Recognising the Internationale Bauausstellung, Berlin as an overriding

ECD Architects 1997

Rolls Crescent

Hulme to Stretford

ECD Architects 1997

Rolls Crescent

influence, the architects aimed to unite disparate zones of the city. The variety of dwelling types, structural forms, colours and textures, from acrylic render to buff brick and steel balustrading, has resulted in a friendly and humane architecture far removed from the sterility of the off-white concrete Crescent Blocks of the 1970s.

ADDRESS Rolls Crescent, Hulme, Manchester M16 [1C 108]
CLIENT North British Housing Association
STRUCTURAL ENGINEER Curtins
CONTRACT VALUE £4,171,171
SIZE 6102 square metres
BUS 17, 114, 115, 290, 291
ACCESS none

ECD Architects 1997

ECD Architects 1997

Manchester Airport

Rail Interchange

This station is among the most structurally and contextually expressive to be built in the 1990s. Described as an 'angular lizard', the Rail Interchange does indeed look like a reptile that has just landed in Manchester Airport's hinterland. Its presence creates a sense of adventure; its form, determined by the need to maximise passenger flows, anticipates the impending journey.

Rising from the station platforms 5 metres below ground, the interchange works on three main levels (an important aspect of the brief). The platforms splay outwards, widening from 6 to 21 metres as they terminate on a split-level concourse. The upper concourse (7 metres above ground level) overlooks the station platforms in one direction and the landside entrance concourse in the other. It links the interchange with the airport terminals via the two tendrils of the travellator (see page 5.10) – phase 1 designed by Aukett. Descending via escalators, stairs or ramps, the lower concourse provides a route to the platforms and marks the semi-circular station entrance hall.

Each level is functionally legible and individually spanned by overlapping wing-like roof decks, reminiscent of aircraft landing flaps. The sense of flight is further emphasised by a pitched spine rooflight. This gradually gains momentum at it travels up the centre of the building, almost appearing to take off at its skyward tip, creating a dynamic relationship with the semi-circular roof of the main entrance.

The view of the skeletal steel and concrete frame over the platforms from the upper concourse is quite dramatic. Connected using a pin-joint structure, the lattice girders under the roofdeck are supported by inclined CHS struts rising from reinforced-concrete columns. In line with the platform edge at concourse level, these columns are set back as the platforms taper inwards, resulting in a 4-metre gap between column and platform

Austin Smith: Lord 1993

Manchester Airport

Austin Smith: Lord 1993

edge. The cantilevered roof canopies shadow the platforms, creating space for passengers to alight and spill out towards the main concourse.

The building materials were chosen to combat the effects of pollution from aviation emissions. Their neutral colours do not interfere with the interchange's structural integrity. The curved roofdeck is stucco-embossed aluminium, here used for low cost and bendability, and bent through two planes to form the semi-circular parasol roof. The entrance hall is glazed from floor to eaves.

This building expresses the excitement of travel, making a dramatic statement in an unremarkable landscape.

ADDRESS Manchester Airport, Manchester [1H 157]
CLIENT Regional Railways North West in conjunction with GMPTE
STRUCTURAL ENGINEER Consultants (BMP) Manchester
CONTRACT £7.2 million
SIZE 2800 square metres
RAIL Manchester Airport
ACCESS open

Austin Smith: Lord 1993

Manchester Airport

Austin Smith: Lord 1993

Manchester Airport Terminal 2

Hardly a soul was to be seen in this place on the grey Sunday afternoon when I visited in April – an atypically quiet moment perhaps considering that Terminal 2 was built to absorb some of the airport's annual 12 million passengers. Unlike the ASL's rail interchange (see page 5.2), whose form creates a sense of activity and movement even when empty, Terminal 2 needs people to bring it to life – the flow of passengers arriving and departing fuels the adrenaline and excitement of travel. At Terminal 2 these activities are cleverly separated to ensure quick and hassle-free passenger movement – made more efficient by legible colour-coded signage – through the building.

Passenger segregation has been achieved by arranging arrivals and departures on different levels. Passengers enter the landside entrance on the upper level where they pass under a space-frame roof into the voluminous space of the check-in hall. Most of the finishes were chosen for durability, easy maintenance, cost-effectiveness and low combustibility; the light-reflective terrazzo floor is a unifying element throughout all the public concourse areas. In the departures concourse this harmonises with the high ceiling and white cladding, while bouncing a mixture of natural and artificial light up to the open-cell non-reflective ceiling.

The light and airy nature of this space is in complete contrast to the airside arrivals. Passengers are lead down a 600-metre pier to immigration control where the low ceiling and overwhelming carpet design combine to make the space dark and oppressive.

Isolated from airside views, the departures concourse is dedicated to shopping and leisure with familiar high-street chains lining the terrazzo street. Once inside the departure lounge the full-height glazing allows plane spotting as an alternative activity to visiting the duty-free shop.

The consistent modularity throughout the building provides a grid for

Scott Brownrigg and Turner 1993

Scott Brownrigg and Turner 1993

Manchester Airport Terminal 2

all building elements, from furniture to floors plinths. All the internal prefabricated cladding panels were selected for flexibility and ease of assembly to meet the schedule – four years from start to finish. At human level these are pink, complemented by purple leather Trax seating in the main departures concourse. The colour scheme throughout was inspired by dilutions of Manchester Airport's red and blue logo. Appointed in February 1989, the architects were responsible for co-ordinating the detail design, principles of which had already been established by the airport's technical services department.

The overall design suffers, like many other international terminals of its type, from a shopping-mall-cum-airport mentality more in tune with commercial flexibility than with creative expression. However, Terminal 2 is a user-friendly building, approached in a practical and functional manner, and deserves to be praised for its efficient layout – the journey through departures averages 25 minutes, with car parking conveniently located adjacent to the terminal building. There is also plenty of space to stretch out should you suffer seasonal delays.

ADDRESS Manchester Airport Terminal 2, Manchester [5H 147]
CLIENT Manchester Airport plc
STRUCTURAL ENGINEER Scott Wilson Kirkpatrick and Partners
SIZE 82,526 square metres
RAIL Manchester Airport
ACCESS landside only

Scott Brownrigg and Turner 1993

Manchester Airport

Scott Brownrigg and Turner 1993

Travellator

Following the expansion of the airport, the travellator was designed to link Terminal 1 with the new rail interchange (see page 5.2). Travelling down this 275-metre tube from the train station feels like going on a lunar journey – it wouldn't look out of place on the set of *2001: A Space Odyssey*, or indeed on the drawing board of Future Systems. Eight metres above ground level and supported by slender concrete columns, on its aerial journey the travellator passes over a clutter of two heavily used roads, a 24-hour bus station and through a multi-storey car park before arriving in the terminal building. Here the tube slots into a new communications tower that houses two hydraulic lifts, escalators and stairs to the arrivals section on the ground floor. Access to departures is via a bridged link that cuts through two decks of the car park. This link forms a new concourse suspended above the car-park approach road, accommodating three 55-person lifts, escalators and stairs.

The fuselage of a Boeing aircraft inspired the travellator's tubular form, its steel frame clad with lightweight aluminium, with glazing allowing views over the airport. Access to air-handling units and the travellator mechanism is via external service hatches, similar to fuel hatches in the undercarriage of an aircraft.

Inside the tube, services are neatly concealed in a suspended ribboned ceiling, referring to an aircraft's overhead hand-luggage storage. This continues down the centre of the travellator's longitudinal plan above the two travellator belts, each the width of two trolleys. Recessed floor lights provide navigation to the travellators like emergency aisle lights, and the futuristic effect is completed by blue neon strip lights shadowing the moving handrails. At both ends the walls of the travellators are punctuated by red and green lights, echoing port and starboard runway lights. Walkways run either side of the travellators, parallel to the glazing.

Aukett 1993

Aukett 1993

Manchester Airport

Travellator

The success of this project was reflected in the completion of Phase 2 of the travellator that links the rail interchange with Terminal 2. Manchester Airport bought the design concept from the architects and is now planning future phases as the tube network provides a faster and more efficient transit system knitting together the distant elements of the airport's infrastructure.

ADDRESS Manchester Airport Terminal 1, Manchester [5H 147]
CLIENT Manchester Airport
STRUCTURAL ENGINEER Travers Morgan
LIGHTING DESIGNER Lighting Design Partnership
RAIL Manchester Airport
ACCESS open

Aukett 1993

Aukett 1993

Northern Quarter to Middleton

Alcohol Information Centre

Historically, the Northern Quarter has strong Italian associations through the people who live, work and play in the area. These are evident on the building's façade which required extensive renovation to restore its original character. During this process the building team unearthed the name 'Henry Jacob' beneath the mortar and paintwork at the top. Rather than remove or hide this, they chose to make it a feature and the restored and repainted façade celebrates its history with 'Henry Jacob' proudly displayed at the top.

The Alcohol Information Centre is a quiet and unassuming building, housed at the bottom of the three-storey structure, featuring a compact reception and consultation rooms. Beneath the Italian façade at street level the architect has installed a new frontage to the centre, providing a discreet barrier to the services offered inside, while also allowing natural light and a sense of activity on the street to filter in.

A new slender timber frame was added to support opaque glazing, providing privacy for client counselling. Interior walls are painted in a variety of refreshing colours, giving an air of informality. Delicate lighting and small fans all create a comfortable atmosphere, helping clients to feel at ease.

ADDRESS 87 Oldham Street, Manchester [4E 95]
CLIENT Alcohol Information Centre
CONTRACT VALUE £60,000
SIZE 150 square metres
METROLINK Piccadilly Gardens
BUS 147, 180, 216, 230, 231, 237
ACCESS reception only

Sagar Stevenson Architects 1998

Northern Quarter to Middleton

Sagar Stevenson Architects 1998

Baguley Court

The clients approached the architects following a recommendation, with a brief to redesign the two main bedrooms of their apartment in suburban Middleton, north of the city centre. One of the smallest projects in this guide, it is a fine example of design on a tight budget and in limited space.

The bedrooms were fundamentally the same with an emphasis on gold and silver metallic finishes, but each with their own character. The first bedroom manages to be both austere and exuberant: painted concrete walls are inset with geometric forms, breaking down expansive planes with visual stimuli and warmth – cobalt, lilac, silver leaf and slate are all used. Brushed angular stainless-steel skirting continues the language of modernity, complementing the geometric forms throughout. Shelving, doors and door furniture fashioned from industrial materials maintain the aesthetic, balanced by soft materials and warm colours. The space is contemporary without a slavish adherence to the dictates of fashion.

In the second bedroom the designer used paint colours – gold, fawn and mustard – usually seen on motor vehicles, complemented by silver leaf, giving definition to the room's character. Voluminous storage is concealed behind gold mirrored doors with quilted stainless-steel panels .

The interior is a fine example of enlightened patronage by clients who knew what they wanted, but were prepared to see their expectations adapted through collaboration with the design team.

ADDRESS Baguley Court, Middleton, Manchester [3C 68]
CLIENTS Simon Derrett and Simon Moseley
BUS 125, 165, 167
ACCESS none

Pocket Rocket 1998

Northern Quarter to Middleton

Pocket Rocket 1998

Café Pop

> Creativity thrives in adversity. Gentrification is the fire blanket of the inspiration inferno. Café society is stifling self-expression with espresso. Planning out poverty and designing for desirables leaves a synthetic society of cultural thrill seekers, buying tickets for the next performance of urban chic revival whilst unwittingly pricing the performers off the stage.
>
> *The Bugle*

This is the passionate voice of Michael Trainer, who with fellow residents started the Northern Quarter Association, a community-led organisation designed to improve the urban environment without destroying its character or cultural identity. Born in north Manchester, Trainer was attracted to the gritty environs of Oldham Street: decaying Victorian buildings, sex shops, and a population of avant-garde retailers that provide the counter-cultural alternative to the Arndale Centre which opened in 1976.

For the last 12 years he has been an inspired collector of twentieth-century design. Particularly interested in plastics, he has a total of 36 collections that narrate the social and cultural history of their time. Among his favourite objects is a 1950s Starr record player, its streamlined form symbolising the twentieth century's obsession with speed.

Ten years ago, to subsidise his collection he opened Design goes Pop, a shop in Afflecks Palace, which sold 'designer junk of the 60s and 70s.' Ahead of its time, the shop was not commercially successful but it did attract interest. This led, five years later, to the opening of Café Pop, emporium of kitsch pop ephemera, also offering affordable veggie fodder. Every surface pays homage to popular design from the 1950s to the 1970s, from Top of the Pops record covers lining one wall to a spherical Sanyo speaker that celebrates the space race. For 30p a 1959 Bal AMI

Michael Trainer 1993

Michael Trainer 1993

Northern Quarter to Middleton

Café Pop

jukebox plays tunes from Hendrix's 'Purple Haze' to Oasis hits – a coincidence as Noel Gallagher of Oasis owns one of Trainer's jukeboxes.

Also lecturing in bad design at Manchester Metropolitan University, Trainer has a Sinclair c5 parked in the café. The example of bad design he uses in his lectures is a tooth-cleaning product from the 1950s. Labelled the 'Water Pik' it is designed to sandblast your teeth – as well as having the potential to give you a nasty electric shock, its high-velocity water jet can decorate your face and bathroom.

Collections like Michael Trainer's are integral to contemporary design theory. Faced with the prospect of having to sell his entire collection, let's hope that, with all the development going on in Manchester and the council's enlightened architectural patronage, a permanent home can be found for this physical thesis. A collection documenting a century of such innovation and design (good and bad) is definitely worth celebrating.

ADDRESS 34–36 Oldham Street, Manchester M1 [4E 95]
METROLINK to Piccadilly Gardens
BUS 147, 180, 216, 230, 231, 237
ACCESS open

Michael Trainer 1993

Northern Quarter to Middleton

Michael Trainer 1993

Commonwealth Stadium

This showpiece stadium is designed to house the 2002 Commonwealth Games and to provide a new home for Manchester City Football Club. Funding came from Manchester City Council (£13 million) and Sport England (£77 million), using National Lottery funds.

Only a mile from the city centre, it will revitalise the neglected eastern side of Manchester. It will be part of the Sportcity complex, linking together the Velodrome, a new all-purpose sports academy, athletics facilities, a national squash headquarters and an in-door tennis centre, effectively turning the area into a centre of sporting excellence.

Twelve massive vertical masts supporting the roof structure will act as a focal point for the Commonwealth Games. Designed to be built in two stages, the first will feature 38,000 seats for spectators watching athletic events, then in the second stage extra seating totalling 48,000 will be added for the new home of Manchester City football club.

When completed, the stadium will be a fitting tribute to the city's aspirations for world recognition as a major sports event provider, with the potential to host the Olympic Games early in the new century. The complex is easily reached from the motorway network and will shortly have a metrolink supertram station as part of the planned £500 million programme announced in March 2000, to be built as soon as possible.

ADDRESS Eastlands, East Manchester
CLIENT Manchester City Council
STRUCTURAL ENGINEERS Ove Arup & Partners
CONTRACT VALUE £90 million
SIZE 48,000 seats
COMPLETION 2002
ACCESS open

Ove Arup and Partners 2002

Commonwealth Stadium

Ove Arup and Partners 2002

Daily Express Building

The Daily Express Building – Manchester's only listed 1930s landmark – has been converted into luxury offices. Built in 1939, it is one of three buildings designed by Sir Owen Williams for Beaverbrook newspapers – the others are located in London's Fleet Street and Glasgow.

The building, now sleek and elegant, is situated to the east of the Northern Quarter and brings life to a particularly run-down and uncompromising part of the city. After Express Newspapers vacated the premises in the 1980s the building was left to decay much like its neighbours – derelict mills and warehouses, the remnants of the textile industry.

The 12-metre-high printing hall, rising from the basement to the second floor, was the original focus of the building. The most challenging aspect of the design was how to insert office accommodation into this space while retaining its spatial clarity. This was achieved by extending an existing first-floor mezzanine across the hall and setting it back 2 metres from the façade, thus giving the impression of internal volume. Another void has been created at the rear of the building by cutting away the floors to form a full-height lightwell, punctuated at fifth-floor level by a glazed-in balcony.

The interior has been completely gutted to install suspended ceilings, access floors, new services, lifts, WCs and means of escape – all the requirements of modern office space. Basement parking, plant, and storage space has been provided by the insertion of a new ground-level floorplate supported by steel columns.

In poor condition, the entire external envelope was renewed, respecting the smooth continuity and glazing lines of Williams' original scheme. The original components of the façade – steel flats, black Vitralight spandrel panels and float glass – have been replaced by a curtain-wall system designed to match the original mullion widths. Grey-tinted

Michael Hyde and Partners 1995

Michael Hyde and Partners 1995

Daily Express Building

glass coated with black film was used to give the appearance of the original Vitralight panels and to comply with building regulations.

The most impressive element of the scheme is the new extension, a seamless addition that reinstates Williams' original concept. This could not be fulfilled at the time because the Express Group could not secure the land on which it stands. Funded by the Express Group and regeneration grants, projects like this are fundamental in the preservation of architectural heritage. The architects have brought this magnificent building back to life and created a landmark within a decaying urban area.

ADDRESS Great Ancoats Street, Manchester [3F 95]
CLIENT The Express Group
STRUCTURAL ENGINEER Sir Robert McAlpine
BUS 23, 24, 74, 147, 165, 182, 188
ACCESS limited

Michael Hyde and Partners 1995

Michael Hyde and Partners 1995

No. 1 Dorsey Street

No. 1 Dorsey Street, with a footprint of more than 420 square metres, is a quiet backwater off Tibb Street, home to 13 recently built flats and three retail units. Situated on a corner site, the development is a welcome contribution to affordable quality housing in the city centre. Mixed-use developments of this calibre, central to the urban-renewal programme, will revitalise the area.

The dominant feature of the development is the use of industrial materials, reflecting Manchester's austerity. The flats are constructed in a rich combination of brickwork and tiles, balanced by steelwork and timber. Dark-blue engineering bricks form a strong base, complemented by a band of mosaic tiling, bringing a sense of solidity to the block at ground- and first-floor levels. Red brickwork above maintains the building's overall integrity. A strong vertical incision with a patterned steel security gate on the Dorsey Street side allows full access. The balconies and other structural steelwork are all detailed in the same manner, adding continuity to the aesthetic of the building. Corners of the block have been sensitively removed, with a strong steel column supporting the balconies, creating a softer and more welcoming appeal.

ADDRESS 1 Dorsey Square, Manchester [3F 95]
CLIENTS Guinness Trust/Tung Sing Housing Association
QUANTITY SURVEYOR Whealing Horton and Toms
CONTRACT VALUE £525,000
SIZE 1220 square metres
METROLINK Piccadilly Gardens
BUS 147, 180, 216, 230, 231, 237
ACCESS none

Sagar Stevenson Architects 1998

Northern Quarter to Middleton

Sagar Stevenson Architects 1998

Dry 201

Manchester has a fine legacy of design-led bars and nightclubs, arguably starting in the 1980s with the Haçienda and Dry 201 for Factory Records. Both interiors were designed by Ben Kelly who has had a long affiliation with the record company. He was also responsible for designing the interior of Factory Records' Charles Street offices and more recently the loft apartment of Antony Wilson, Factory Records' legendary founder (see page 1.24). It is not surprising, then, that Kelly comes from a generation of designers influenced by the music industry. His contemporaries include Peter Saville (with whom Kelly won a D&AD award in 1981, for Orchestral Manoeuvres in the Dark's perforated album cover) and graphic designer Neville Brody, whose post-punk eclecticism and Industria typeface is perhaps best commemorated in *The Face*, which spearheaded a new genre in consumer magazines.

Completed in 1989, Dry 201 (its name derived from Factory Records' unique cataloguing system) was originally conceived as a pre-club bar to visit before moving on to the Haçienda. Manchester's most seminal and notorious venue, the Haçienda was famous for promoting some of Factory Records' most successful bands, from New Order (who were co-investors in Dry 201) to the Happy Mondays, who spearheaded the emergence of the 'Madchester' scene. It was also associated with the birth of 'acid house', which became an unfortunate catalyst in the club's eventual closure in early 1998.

With the exception of Antony Wilson's apartment, Dry 201 is now the only active representation of Ben Kelly's design in the city. Situated at the top of Oldham Street, the bar occupies a former furniture showroom in the heart of the Northern Quarter. Dry 201 is a considerable size – 450 metres long and with a capacity of 500 – dwarfing most bars nearby. The interior boasts one of the longest bars in Manchester: 24 metres, and clad

Ben Kelly Design (BKD) 1989

Ben Kelly Design (BKD) 1989

Dry 201

in tough stainless steel. Telegraph poles provide a sense of order in the central area, and mark the junctions with diagonal leaning bars, in what is a very public space. More intimate areas with softer furnishings are provided at the back of the bar and at the front next to the full-height window. Exposed I-beams and minimal industrial lighting project an austere feeling, softened by the use of warm materials in the timber flooring and Jasper Morrison furniture.

Vibrant and playful colours are Ben Kelly's trademark, and here he has used them to great effect, bringing a richness to an interior that could otherwise have been sterile. The wall of blue glazed tiles on the external façade is another Ben Kelly motif, also expressed on the external walls of the Haçienda.

If you only have the time to visit one bar in Manchester, go to Dry 201. Like its sister venue the Haçienda, Dry 201 was revolutionary in its time and was the birthplace of the continental bar culture in the city. Still contemporary today, its expression epitomises Manchester's industrial character; it has spawned many imitations but these have never quite matched the originality or ingenuity of the original scheme.

ADDRESS Oldham Street, Manchester [4E 95]
CLIENTS Factory Records/New Order
SIZE 779 square metres
METROLINK Piccadilly Gardens
BUS 147, 180, 216, 230, 231, 237
ACCESS open

Ben Kelly Design (BKD) 1989

Ben Kelly Design (BKD) 1989

The National Cycling Centre

To the north of the city centre, the National Cycling Centre, opened in 1994, is Britain's first purpose-built cycling stadium, also housing the British Cycling Federation headquarters. The centre will play an important role when Manchester hosts the 2002 Commonwealth Games.

The centre started its life on the drawing board of architects HOK who designed the overall concept; it was constructed as a design and build project by AMEC.

The form of the building was determined by the highly complex cycling track, designed by R V Webb Ltd. The track is 7 metres wide and 250 metres long, constructed from Siberian pine and contoured to provide a surface for international-standard indoor cycling. Another significant factor dictating the building's form, particularly the roof, was the structural steelworks and fabrication of the complex 3D forms. The architect points out that 'there is a clear analogy with modern cycle technology and in particular the form of the cyclist's helmet.' Silver cladding and blue engineering bricks complement its dynamic form.

The building is restrained and elegant, a subtle backdrop for the spectacle inside.

ADDRESS [3C 96]
CLIENT Manchester City Council
STRUCTURAL ENGINEER Watson Steel
CYCLE TRACK DESIGN R V Webb Limited
CONTRACT VALUE £9.0 million
SIZE 10,000 square metres
BUS 171, 216, 230–237
ACCESS check before visiting

Faulkner Browns 1994

Northern Quarter to Middleton

Faulkner Browns 1994

Smithfield Buildings

Loft living, a concept developed by struggling artists in Manhattan in the 1930s, has now become a fashionable way to live. Providing a focus for regeneration, Smithfield Buildings promotes mixed-use and sustainability, bringing a new wave of design-conscious individuals into the heart of the city.

Situated in Oldham Street opposite Dry 201 and Café Pop (see pages 6.18 and 6.6), Smithfield Buildings was once home to Affleck and Brown, the 'Harrods of the North' which opened at the turn of the last century. Affleck and Brown occupied a prominent position in what was, until the opening of the Arndale Centre in 1976, Manchester's prime shopping district. Still boasting many shops and a lively street culture, the area is a vibrant and somewhat bohemian place in which to live, close to some of Manchester's oldest venues, such as Band on the Wall. English Partnerships, keen to embrace this vitality and to use the project as a catalyst for future redevelopment, provided grant aid.

Four storeys high, the building now houses retail units (mainly fronting Oldham Street) on the ground floor and 81 apartments on the upper floors. The entrance to the apartments is on Tibb Street, its cast-iron construction reminiscent of the nineteenth-century buildings in SoHo, New York. Contrasting with the brickwork of the adjacent façades, windows are set back from balconies and are contained behind the full-height cast-iron framework. The street entrance is clearly identified by the contemporary treatment of these elements and declares the building's new use. Once inside, a 10-metre-high void contains the stair and glass-backed lift to the residential floors. Its walls are pigmented with a deep red, continuing the external language, and are adorned with MDF letter boxes that sit flush with the wall.

Celebrating the building's existing structure and deep plan, the archi-

Stephenson Bell 1997

Stephenson Bell 1997

tects have arranged the apartments around two lightwells (now atriums), one remodelled from an existing arcade. This has enabled the apartments to be double aspect, with living space to the street side and sleeping areas to the atrium side. Toilets, kitchens, and storage space are arranged centrally in each plan.

The atrium spaces are beautifully designed, with access to apartments via an internal street, each level linked by a stairway. Blissfully calm, these spaces leave a lasting impression. Exposed brickwork is highlighted by white plaster and softened by timber flooring. The existing pitch-pine floor has been retained and reinstated in the balustrading, with the timber slats arranged like horizontal fencing; giant palms and pebble beds form the central garden, the tree branches stretching up towards the glass pitched roof.

Car parking lies in a building adjacent to the Tibb Street entrance, linked to Smithfield Buildings via a covered walkway. Each side of the bridged link is covered by graphics designed by a local artist.

The majority of apartments were sold – for between £65,000 and £300,000 – off the plans. This is hardly surprising. With design-led developers and award-winning architects, Smithfield Buildings has to be a precedent for modern living.

ADDRESS Tibb Street, Manchester [4E 95]
CLIENT Urban Splash
STRUCTURAL ENGINEER Eric Bassett Associates
CONTRACT VALUE £6.5 million
METROLINK Piccadilly Gardens
BUS 147, 180, 216, 230, 231, 237
ACCESS none

Stephenson Bell 1997

Stephenson Bell 1997

The Big Issue in the North

The northern headquarters of *The Big Issue* is located at the far end of Oldham Street towards Ancoats, easily reached on foot from Piccadilly.

The client wanted maximum transparency throughout the refurbished building so that the vendors can see the staff going about their work and *vice versa*. Costs had to be kept to a minimum.

All the floors have been stripped back to form a massive atrium space at the front, creating a greater degree of visibility, exposing structural supports, and allowing natural light to permeate the interior space. Large areas of glazing provide some privacy to the open-plan offices. Space has been allocated for an in-house doctor's surgery, employment unit, laundrette, showers and toilets. The harshness of industrial light fittings has been tempered by clever detailing. Removal of suspended ceilings increased room volumes and reduced costs. A steel staircase allows efficient circulation and creates a sense of drama in the central space.

The Big Issue headquarters building is commendable for two reasons: it proves that good design need not be expensive; and it is a strong statement of the client's commitment to creating a building that serves the needs of the magazine's vendors.

ADDRESS 135–141 Oldham Street, Manchester [3F 95]
CLIENT The Big Step
STRUCTURAL ENGINEER Eric Bassett Associates
QUANTITY SURVEYOR Simon Fenton Partnership
CONTRACT VALUE £828,000
METROLINK Piccadilly Gardens
BUS 147, 180, 216, 230, 231, 237
ACCESS front lobby only

Ian Simpson Architects 1998

The Big Issue in the North

Northern Quarter to Middleton

Ian Simpson Architects 1998

The Buddhist Centre

Just as through meditation awareness penetrates deeper and deeper
into the rotten layers of views, attitudes, and reactions, so we dug
deeper into the rotten roof timbers, crumbling brickwork and infected
window frames ... Through raising awareness of the building's original
structure and concerns, and then embellishing it with original western
Buddhist artwork, the design itself could provide an example on the
material plane of conversion and renewal – towards which on a spiritual plane all Buddhists aspire.
The Buddhist Centre, Manchester

This quotation represents the faith and determination that went into the
transformation of a decaying cotton warehouse into what is now Europe's
largest urban Buddhist centre. The regeneration project, which became
a metaphor for Buddhist beliefs, was co-ordinated by Buddhist Mokshapriya, and most of the building work was carried out over 18 months
by fellow Buddhists and volunteers. Having outgrown their previous
premises, the Buddhists decided to relocate to the cheap and central
Northern Quarter. Acquisition and development of the building
happened through coincidence. Mokshapriya met architect Dominic
Sagar, a member of the Northern Quarter Association and actively
involved in the area's regeneration. He became responsible for obtaining
planning permission and generating 75 per cent of the project's funding,
from the European Development Fund (for business fit-out and refurb),
English Heritage (external cleaning and renovation), and an arts grant
(external railings and security).

With the help of architect Tony Mead (responsible for space planning),
the Buddhists sandblasted the walls and stripped down the woodwork. One
of the most impressive features is an existing timber stair, linking a café and

Mokshapriya with Dominic Sagar and Tony Mead 1995

Mokshapriya with Dominic Sagar and Tony Mead 1995

bookshop; the building also houses a shrine and meditation rooms; meeting rooms, library and alternative health centre; a video production unit and women's DTP group; and a communal apartment for seven.

All the materials were reclaimed; they include maple-strip flooring from a school gym and radiators from a hospital, and the copper and brass used on the door to the main shrine room. Influenced by the palette of Dry 201 (see page 6.18), Mokshapriya chose colours to promote a sense of well-being. The soft green of the planar walls in the café/bookshop together with a water feature create a relaxing environment, a contrast to the surroundings of the Northern Quarter. A freestanding blue curved wall behind a gold Buddha in a shrine room represents the sky, a common image in meditation practice.

All the ironmongery, signage and sculptures were designed by Buddhist artists. The floral security grills of the front elevation depict the journey of self-discovery from chaos (represented by wavy lines at the bottom) to enlightenment (represented by an open lotus flower at the top). An angel in the bookshop, created from scrap metal by Buddhist Sahaja, is a symbol of renewal.

This project is a remarkable example of community-led regeneration, where parties have shared goals and values. It is a pity that commercial development cannot benefit from the same philosophy.

ADDRESS 16–20 Turner Street, Manchester M4 [3E 95]
CLIENT Manchester Buddhist Society
CONTRACT VALUE £250,000
SIZE 1860 square metres
METROLINK Piccadilly Gardens BUS 147, 180, 216, 230, 231, 237
ACCESS open

Mokshapriya with Dominic Sagar and Tony Mead 1995

Northern Quarter to Middleton

Mokshapriya with Dominic Sagar and Tony Mead 1995

Love Saves the Day

Located beneath the newly developed Smithfield Buildings (see page 6.24), Love Saves the Day is a recent addition to the growing urban community of the Northern Quarter. The clients, Becky Jones and Chris Joyce (ex-Simply Red drummer), wanted to create a retail outlet with a cosmopolitan slant, that would reflect their passion for food. The result is a one-stop convenience store offering a wide range of continental food, a deli and an off-licence.

Branding and graphic design are integral to the store's identity. Local designers Via Communications have provided striking images and pictograms to help shoppers navigate throughout the store.

Walls stripped back to brick and rough plywood sheeting form a textured backdrop to the deli. Food-storage and display units are mostly fixed at at the perimeter, freeing floor space at the heart of the shop. Rubber-granule flooring is intended to give an impression of austerity, brrowed from comparable delis overseas – its sucess in this is debatable.

Love Saves the Day is an honest attempt to provide a new style of retailing in Manchester – but do the people want it?

ADDRESS Smithfield Buildings, Tibb Street, Manchester [4E 95]
CLIENT LStD Limited
SIZE 170 square metres
METROLINK Market Street
ACCESS open
BUS 147, 180, 216, 230, 231, 237

Judge Gill Associates 1999

Ancoats Urban Village

Ancoats – a cotton-processing suburb to the north-east of Manchester city centre, adjacent to the Northern Quarter – was at the epicentre of the industrial revolution, a nineteenth-century equivalent of Silicon Valley. However, since the area's decline from the 1960s, the result of deindustrialisation, theft, vandalism and arson have plagued it. The Anglo-Italian community that once populated the area, providing its rich and diverse character, has mostly moved on, leaving a shell, its former glory and community spirit gone.

In 1994 Manchester City Council finally attempted to tackle the decline and the structural problems of the area. In 1995 the Ancoats Building Preservation Trust and the Ancoats Urban Village Company were formed. One of their first missions was to save key historic buildings, notably St Peter's Church and Murray's Mill. Their overall aim is to transform Ancoats, enhancing the existing infrastructure and renewing the area as the first 'urban village' of the millennium, with a resurgent multicultural vitality.

St Peter's, now owned by the Buildings Preservation Trust, had been badly damaged by fire. It has now been partially renovated and its Italianate structure forms the area's heart. Appropriately, the church will stand on a corner of a piazza, a space for people to meet and socialise. The 'dark satanic mills' will be refurbished and developed as apartments, offices, shops and bars. At the time of writing (summer 1999) Ancoats (with Castlefield and Worsley) has been shortlisted as a possible World Heritage Site, testament to the importance of the place and the commitment of the volunteers who have recognised its significance and potential.

ACCESS due to be developed in 2002

Ian Finlay Architects/Paul Butler Associates 1995–

Ian Finlay Architects/Paul Butler Associates 1995–

Salford Quays to Lower Broughton

Centenary Building, University of Salford

The University of Salford's Centenary Building is situated next to the Adelphi Building, in the post-industrial hinterland of Salford. The building is a tribute to the ingenuity of the architect – the original brief was drastically reworked during construction to accommodate design students as opposed to the product designers and engineers initially envisaged as occupants.

The building's two parts are connected by an atrium 'street', creating a vibrant social space with views into the adjoining studios. The front section, three floors of studio space complete with a glazed façade, makes a strong visual impact on the landscape. The use of industrial materials and minimal colour create an air of austerity in keeping with the surrounding area. The rear building, clad in stainless steel, presents a defensive face towards the adjacent housing estates. Glass bricks and smooth concrete finishes are durable and minimise maintenance costs.

This is a no-nonsense functionalist building, achieved within a tight budget and an even tighter timescale, capturing the spirit of the early modernist masters.

ADDRESS Adelphi Street, Salford [3B 94]
CLIENT University of Salford
STRUCTURAL ENGINEER SMP/Atelier One
BUS 294, 692
RAIL Salford
ACCESS none

Hodder Associates 1996

Centenary Building, University of Salford

Salford Quays to Lower Broughton

Hodder Associates 1996

Imperial War Museum (North)

The Imperial War Museum (North) will be Daniel Libeskind's second major project to be built in the UK. With a reputation for designing controversial and complex buildings, his other museums include the Jewish Museum in Berlin and the forthcoming 'spiral' extension to London's V&A. Libeskind's proposal for the museum was selected from a strong field of entrants and its choice demonstrates Salford City Council's determination to foster innovative architectural design.

The museum will be located opposite Michael Wilford's The Lowry (see page 7.6) and together these buildings will constitute an important centre for the arts. The client anticipates that the new building will attract more than 400,000 visitors a year, providing a boost to an area overburdened with commercial postmodern developments.

The underlying concept for the museum will be the 'shattered globe' of the fragile Earth whose shards represent the cultures and lives lost and destroyed in global conflict. This powerful imagery is the starting point for the museum's disorientated form and dynamic spatial arrangement. The broken pieces of the globe enclose the building's activities, defining its overall footprint.

ADDRESS Salford Quays [1G 107]
CLIENT Imperial War Museum
EXHIBITION DESIGN DEGW/Amalgam
CONTRACT VALUE £35 million
BUS 52, 69, 89, 294, M11
ACCESS to be confirmed

Daniel Libeskind 2002

Daniel Libeskind 2002

The Lowry

L S Lowry (1887–1976) is best remembered for his paintings of the bleak industrial landscape in and around Salford; the matchstick figures that occupy them have become a trademark. The centre, adjacent to the Manchester Ship Canal, is one of the few landmark buildings in the north-west that has received substantial funding from the Millennium Commission, the Heritage Lottery Fund and the Arts Council of England.

Dedicated to the performing and visual arts, the centre features the 1730-seat Lyric Theatre and the adaptable 450-seat Quays Theatre, with dressing rooms and rehearsal facilities. Art galleries will display the city's celebrated collection of Lowry's paintings and provide flexible space for exhibitions. With a purpose-built public plaza to the front of the building, the Lowry will help to bring a community spirit to the area.

The second phase of the Metrolink will connect the arts centre to Manchester, allowing easy access to the canal basin complex and café-bars. The Lowry provides a unique focal point to a once-neglected area of the city.

ADDRESS Salford Quays [1G 107]
CLIENT Salford City Council
STRUCTURAL ENGINEER Buro Happold
BUS 52, 69, 89, 294, M11
ACCESS to be confirmed

Michael Wilford & Partners 2000

Michael Wilford & Partners 2000

Trafford Park

North Stand, Old Trafford

Enter the theatre of dreams and you may well witness a Manchester United victory – just like I did when I watched the Reds thrash Charlton Athletic 4:1. An emotional match.

The North Stand demolishes the contention that, since the abolition of the terraces following the Hillsborough disaster, the glory and camaraderie has gone out of football. Not a chance. Justly proud of its past and its well-documented successes, the richest football club in Europe has built one of the largest stands in the UK, bringing the total seating capacity at Old Trafford up to 55,000. The North Stand, a huge triple-deck exoskeletal structure, has the same area as the pitch and a capacity of 26,000. Its cantilevered decks gape open like a huge mouth, ready to roar as Yorke scores the first goal for United.

Rising 45 metres above the pitch, the steel-framed stand was positioned so that it does not cast any shadows over the players, and it provides fans with an unimpeded view of the pitch. This was achieved by building beyond the original site perimeter – over United Road and on to a former industrial estate that United bought for a tidy £9.1 million (a mere 1.5 players). Accommodation is arranged over three tiers; these are divided into eight seating levels accessed via escalators or lifts, with the top tier angled at 34 degrees above the horizontal and the second at 30 degrees.

Behind the seating is a new bar, the Red Café, and a club museum dedicated to the history and achievements of Manchester United, from its humble beginnings as Newton Heath in 1878 to the Premier League victory in 1997. The most significant, and somewhat tragic, exhibit is a memorial to Sir Matt Busby and the Busby Babes, eight of whom died in the Munich air crash of 1958. The memorial display includes the original clock from outside the ground that apparently stopped forever at the

Atherden Fuller 1998

Atherden Fuller 1998

time of the crash.

Manchester United is a hugely important part of Mancunian culture. Having produced some of the most legendary players of modern times – from Bobby Charlton and George Best to Eric Cantona and Ryan Giggs – the passionate loyalty of the club's fans is hardly surprising. During the match I watched, this patronage was humorously demonstrated when one fan proudly streaked across the pitch in protest at the eventually repulsed Rupert Murdoch take-over bid.

ADDRESS Sir Matt Busby Way, Trafford Park, Manchester [2F 107]
CLIENT Manchester United Football Club
STRUCTURAL ENGINEER Campbell Reith Hill
CONTRACT VALUE £18.65 million
METROLINK Old Trafford
BUS 114, 230, 252–257, 263, 264
ACCESS open (via Old Trafford Stadium Tours)

Atherden Fuller 1998

North Stand, Old Trafford

Trafford Park

Atherden Fuller 1998

Trafford Centre

Manchester's Trafford Park was one of the first industrial estates in the world, created more than 100 years ago when the region was devoted to manufacturing and industrial production. Second only in size to the mighty Ruhr region in Germany, Trafford Park had more than 500,000 people working within its factories between the world wars.

The recently completed Trafford Centre is a staggering £600 million retail and leisure development, employing more than 7000 people with another 500 employed at the nearby sports complex. It boasts 280 retail units, totalling three miles of shop fronts and the first Selfridges outside London; an estimated 500,000 people visit the centre every week.

The centre's 'themed' shopping areas create the Egypt, Venice, New Orleans and China 'experiences' in Trafford Park. Large sarcophagi line the walls in the Egyptian area, where the toilets are decorated with hieroglyphics. Jungles, jazz, tombs and treasures are all devalued in this massive theme park – the perfect environment for lovers of kitsch.

This architecture of perversity completely disregards the area's industrial heritage. An alien being on the Mancunian landscape, the development appears to have been artificially transplanted on to its present site. Already heavily criticised as a paean to the trivial and banal, the Trafford Centre can be described as the meeting point between Michael Graves and Norman Bates. Not a shopping experience for the faint-hearted.

ADDRESS Dumplington, Trafford Park [1G 105 and 1F 105]
CLIENT Peel Holdings
CONTRACT VALUE £600 million
BUS 54, 100, 241, 243, 270, 272, 294, 297, 500 (Barton Dock Road)
ACCESS open

Chapman Taylor Partners 1998

Chapman Taylor Partners 1998

Index

Manchester: a guide to recent architecture

Index

All pictures by Keith Collie except:
page 1.25 Ben Kelly Design
page 2.35 Manchester City Council
page 2.37 Michael Hopkins and Partners
page 4.11 Mills Beaumont Leavey
  Channon
page 6.11 Ove Arup and Partners
page 7.5 Daniel Libeskind
page 7.7 The Lowry

Manchester: a guide to recent architecture